Starquill International proudl

Brian Wizard's

NIGERIAN

419

Scam

"GAME OVER!"

Printing history: This copy of Brian Wizard's *Nigerian 419 Scam "Game Over!"* is from the first printing of the first edition.

Published by Starquill International, a division of Brian Wizard's Inc.
Send all correspondence to:

Brian Wizard's Inc.
P.O.Box 42
Wallowa, Oregon 97885
or
www.brianwizard.com

ISBN 0 949702 17 X

Printed at Sheridan Books.
Edited by Marsha Calhoun.

Special Thanks to:
Coordinator: The 419 Coalition, Vanguard News, PanaAfrican News Agency, Global Travller, Western Union, and British Midland, Josi James, and the people of the world who follow my advice regarding their efforts to fight the Nigerian 419 Scam.

For other books, videos and artwork from Brian Wizard, please visit our website: http://www.brianwizard.com.

PREFACE

The term 419 (four-one-nine) comes from the section of the Nigerian criminal code outlawing fraudulent activities. It has become a part of everyday Nigerian language. As others might say that one has cheated, or stolen, or tricked, or misrepresented, or lied, or conned, etc., a Nigerian will often just use the term "419" to cover all or some of the above activities. This book is an entertaining look at Black Currency 419 operations. Black Currency 419 is actually an updated version of the centuries-old West African con called the Red Mercury scam, in which a special chemical is "necessary" to "clean" (ostensible) bank notes, which have been defaced, in order to make them negotiable. Of course, there is always a problem with the supply of the chemical or with the chemical itself, so the bad guys need money from the target in order to get the job done.

Black Currency 419 is the second most prevalent version of the Nigerian Scam. Nigerian 419 operations have been running since at least the mid-1980s and conservative estimates of total monies stolen worldwide through 2000 range from $5 billion on up. That's billion with a B. The United States alone has confirmed losses of $100 million per annum, and estimated losses of $300 plus million per annum, according to the U.S. government. And that's just the U.S., there is of course the rest of the world to factor in as well. It has been publicly reported that according to diplomatic sources in Nigeria, Nigerian 419 operations are the third to fifth largest industry in the country. More information on Nigerian 419 operations is available in the Postscript following the story.

Coordinator, The 419 Coalition
http://home.rica.net/alphae/419coal/
June 2000

I dedicate this book to the people targeted by the 419 scamsters who, after reading this book, decide not to participate. Simply reply to your 419 Scam operative, "Thanks, but no thanks. I read the book."

PROLOGUE

Hello, Brian Wizard here. I am very happy that you are reading this book. I hope this reading experience will entertain you, and at the same time educate you, especially if you are presently in the cross hairs of the Nigerian 419 Scam industry.

Have you received any unsolicited faxes, e-mails, or letters from any African country announcing that someone, somewhere has millions of dollars *for you?* If that is the case, then I am sure that you have many questions. I hope to answer some of those questions for you by sharing my experience of allowing myself to become a victim of the Nigerian 419 Scam. In turn, reading this story could save you a lot of time, trouble, worry, friendships, family quarrels and *money.* I emphasized *money* because that is all the scamsters are after: your hard-earned money, and a lot of it.

Even if you are not an immediate target of the Nigerian 419 Scam, one day you will either be a target, or you will know of someone who has become a target of the scam and its lure of immediate wealth. No matter what, please continue reading. The more people who know about the Nigerian 419 Scam and refuse to participate in its deceit and trickery, the more quickly and effectively we, the honest, hard-working people of the world, can stand up and fight it. The Nigerian 419 Scam is *not* a good thing. In my opinion, the world can do without it.

My goal, as a writer, is to portray the truth through fiction. This approach to storytelling makes the process easier for me, and more entertaining for you. When I became a target of the Nigerian 419 Scam, my investigation into the scam showed me a practice that was unjust, unfair and completely uncalled for. I soon decided to stand up and be counted as an anti-419-scam activist. I hope you will join me in this fight and spread the word: *Do not get involved with the Nigerian 419 Scam!*

So, let's begin this tale of international intrigue and adventure:

I have a small office, in a small town, where the early-morning fog hangs in the air more days than not. That is why my workdays start late, around noon. I live above the valley and its fog, on a hilltop that provides me with an airplane's view of the world below.

In this day and age of high-tech communications, a guy like me doesn't have to go anywhere but an office like mine to feel the pulse of the world. I could work at home, but I find that I work better if I have to get up and go somewhere to focus on the intricate details of my job. In my case, this is usually the research aspect of creative writing. I like to consider myself an investigative novelist. As you will find by reading my other stories, each tale has taken me into a hands-on investigation of some sort of unusual activity. Furthermore, I like the commute. It gets me out of the house, gives me an opportunity to see the beauty of my surroundings as I drive through the picture-perfect landscape, which on the way home includes my estate. I also see more of the wildlife as I drive slowly along the winding roads of the forest. In the end, I love the part about coming home.

In the small and cluttered confines of my downtown communication center you will find all the latest forms of global access: television, radio (AM/FM and short-wave), fax, phone, snail-mail, the internet and e-mail. It's through these links to the outside world that unsolicited communications can be delivered.

Especially junk e-mail. It's through the junk e-mail that anyone can send scams. Sure, you'll get the occasional scam thrown at you by friends and family members who want your money for nothing more than their need to see your love for them.

Then there are the professional scam artists who lure you into high hopes of prosperity:

"Give us your money and we'll sell your products through our website" is a common internet scam. In actuality, these e-mail scamsters take your money, put you and a million other suckers onto their websites in order to cover their overhead expenses, and in the end do little or nothing for you.

"Give us your money, and we'll set you up with a fast and easy money-making business that you can operate at home, in your spare time. Soon, you will be able to quit your day job and retire early from the normal grind. Be your own boss!" is another scam come-on. In the end, you find that you have spent a fair amount of money to work overtime in exchange for an ephemeral hope of early retirement. Once again, reality lowers your high hopes, and you're still at your day job, still looking at a distant date of retirement.

This story is about the time I received unsolicited communications that originated from unknown and ambiguous characters in a far-away place emphatically stating that some people in Nigeria, of all places, desperately needed my help. As a reward, they would transfer a large amount of money into my personal bank account, of which a hefty percentage would have *my name on it*.

FIRST CONTACT

One early September day I entered my office around noon, as per usual, after the sun had dissipated the fog and warmed the air inside my communication center. Life had returned to its ho-hum routine. My last excursion into the combat fray of a full-on international investigation for the purpose of research had ended over three months ago. That investigation took me back to Viet Nam. I needed to research how the people were getting along twenty-five years after the war had ended. Having been a participant in that war, the trip served as a platform for some serious self-exploration. By this time, the excitement had worn off and the mundane blahs of life in the slow lane had again corrupted my preferred mood of suspense and anticipation. My imagination stirred when I opened my e-mail and read the following communiqué:

mohammed abacha,9/8/99 7:47 PM +0100,RE ; BUSINESS   PREPOSITION   1

```
X-From_: abacham@yahoo.com  Wed Sep  8 11:43:31 1999
Date: Wed, 8 Sep 1999 11:47:29 -0700 (PDT)
From: mohammed abacha <abacham@yahoo.com>
Subject: RE ; BUSINESS      PREPOSITION
To: bwizard@eoni.com
MIME-Version: 1.0

ATTN; Brian Wizard

I AM MOHAMMED ABACHA THE SON OF GENERAL SANNI ABACHA WHO WAS
NIGERIA'SHEAD OF STATE UNTIL JUNE 8, 1998,  WHEN HE DIED MY FATHERS
FORTUNE PRESENTLY IS SCATTERED IN MAJOR FINANCIAL REGIONS IN THE WORLD
AND ISBEING INVESTIGATED.
THE PRESENT GOVERNMENT OF NIGERIA IS ALSO HOUNDING MY FAMILY AT HOME
WILLINGLY, MY FAMILY HAS RELINGUISED TO THE GOVERNMENT IN CASH OVER
US$I BILLION APART FROM PROPERTIES.
```

AT THE MOMENT, MY FAMILY IS STILL HOLDING IN SAFE CUSTODY OVER
US$500MILLION, SOME STILL IN NIGERIA, IN SAFE ACCOUNT IN BOTH
COMMERCIAL BANKS AND FINANCIAL HOUSES.MY FAMILY HAS AGREEMENT IN
PRINCIPLE WITH THESE FINANCIAL INSTITUITIONS THAT IF WE CAN FIND A
RELIABLE RECEIVER ABROAD, THEY WILL AID US IN TRANSFERRING THE MONEY
OUT IN BITS FOR REASONS STATED ABOVE, WE ARE
CONTACTING YOU WITH THE HOPE THAT YOU WILL BE AGREEABLE TO OUR
PROPOSAL.

I GOT YOUR CONTACT THROUGH NIGERIA CHAMBER OF COMMERCE AND INDUSTRY.

FOR YOUR WILLINGNESS TO ASSIST US, WE ARE READY TOREWARD YOU AFTER THE
HAS BEEN TRANSFER INTO YOUR AD ACCOUNT ABROAD.

THIS BUSINESS REQUIRES ABSOLUTE TRUST ON YOUR PART BECAUSE MY FAMILY IS
BEING RESTRICTED TO TRAVEL OUT NIGERIA WITH OUR PASSPORT CONFISTICATED
BY THE GOVERNMENT.

CONFIDENCE AND UTMOST SECRECY IS THE WATCHWORD FOR THESE TRANSACTION
AND IF STRICTLY ADHERED TO, IT IS ABSOLUTE RISK FREE.

YOU SHOULD SEND YOUR REPLY TO MY PRIVATE EMAIL ADDRESS WHERE I WILL
LINK YOU WITH A LOCAL ATTORNEY THAT WILL STATE OUT TO YOU THE MODE OF
OPERATIONS, ALSO INCLUDE YOUR PRIVATE TEL/FAX NUMBERS.

PLEASE TREAT AS URGENT AND REPLY EITHER NEGATIVE OR POSITIVE.

MEANWHILE, I THANK YOU IN ADVANCE IN ANTICIPATION OF YOUR CO-OPERATION.

MOHAMMED ABACHA.

"Hmmm," I hummed with wonderment. "This sounds interesting. A *'business preposition.'*" While reading the e-mail I made verbal comments such as, "*Nigerian Head of State. Scattered fortune.* Found my name in the *Nigerian Chamber of Commerce.* What the hell was it doing in there?"

"*Reward* me?" That sounded good. "*Trust, confidence and utmost secrecy?*" That's not quite my forte. I'm a novelist, not a priest.

"*Risk free.*" That sounded too good to be true, plus a bit boring.

What could I do but reply positively?

Dear Mohammed (May I call you Mo?),
It would be my pleasure to assist you. I stand ready to receive your instructions.

Yours truly,
Brian Wizard

I went about my daily routine thereafter, and waited for Mo's reply.

*   *   *

I began the next business day reading Mo's quick reply. I thought he must have been kidding and nothing would come back.

mohammed abacha,9/9/99 2:42 PM -0700,Re: RE ; BUSINESS   PREPOSITIO   1

```
X-From_: abacham@yahoo.com  Thu Sep  9 14:38:06 1999
Date: Thu, 9 Sep 1999 14:42:52 -0700 (PDT)
From: mohammed abacha <abacham@yahoo.com>
Subject: Re: RE ;  BUSINESS      PREPOSITION
To: bwizard@eoni.com
MIME-Version: 1.0

FROM, M, ABACHA.

TO, MR, BRIAN WIZARD.

DEAR, BRIAN  I AM IN RECEIPT OF YOUR MAIL.
I WILL WANT CONTACT MY FAMILY ATTORNEY  DAVID  OLATUNDE ON TELL/FAX NO,
234-1-2660970 FROM THE HOURS OF 2PM TO 5PM NIGERIAN TIME SINCE HE HAD
SUBMITTED YOUR NAME TO THE BANK CONCERND FOR ONWARD APROVAL. DO CALL
HIM FOR MORE BRIFEING.

THANKS AND GOD BLESSING.
```

I don't have many people in my life. That's one reason I talk to myself, I suppose. I have no wife, no kids, no distant relatives who care to visit on a regular basis. Most of my social contact comes through the external communications available in my office, and the people I meet working at their jobs in the various local commercial establishments.

I do have Martin. He's a hardworking outdoorsman. He's a logger by trade, in his mid-thirties, fifteen years my junior. Martin lives next door to my office. He's good for several weekly visits. Martin lives a normal workaday life. He has a family, a couple of dogs, a cat, and several fish in a tank. He loves to hunt, fish, and wander through the wilderness on horseback. He truly is a woodsman. We live similar lifestyles except when it comes to business and hobbies. Our differences give each of us something interesting to talk about. I regale Martin with my international adventures, intrigue, and investigations, while Martin tells me hunting, fishing, logging, and outdoorsman stories.

"Yo," Martin called out, as he walked through my office doorway. "Got anything new cooking in the investigative pot?" He was aware that I had been in a lull.

When I turned to him, after reading my e-mail again to copy down the Nigerian phone number, I announced, "I've got a nibbler at the hook," using Martin's fishing slang. I pantomimed toying with an imaginary fish investigating the bounty attached to my line. "All I need to do to set the hook is make a phone call to Nigeria."

"Do it," Martin encouraged.

I looked at the clock on the wall. It was late afternoon. I had spent most of the day cutting firewood. That sent me to town later than normal. "The people in Nigeria must be a half-day ahead of us."

Martin only nodded, then looked at my bookcase in search of the World Atlas. "Where in Africa?"

"Nigeria. About midway up the left side," I explained, having already researched the location. I picked up the telephone and called the operator. "What's the time difference between Pacific time and Nigerian time?"

"Nine hours," the operator replied.

A quick deduction made it almost midnight in Lagos, Nigeria. "Too late to call. I'll try Saturday morning," I told Martin. "I've got to come to town early to pick up some used windows."

*   *   *

Saturday morning I went to town early, as planned. I picked up the used windows from an old house that was being torn down. I had a new construction project at home: a greenhouse. I was curious to find out if this Nigerian guy David worked on Saturdays. When I entered my office I experienced a sensation I like: butterflies fluttering in my stomach. I was about to yank the line to see if I could set my hook into a story-fish worth further research and investigation.

My office was cold. I turned on the heater. The computer doesn't like to be turned on under fifty degrees. It was forty-eight. I don't like to operate under fifty degrees, either, so I walked over to Martin's house to wait for my office to warm up. Martin's wife, Debbie, offered me breakfast. I accepted.

My upcoming phone call excited Martin. "If they want you to go to Africa, you going to go?" he asked.

"Maybe. I need to do some research first. I believe some parts of Africa are still fairly primitive," I responded.

After breakfast, I returned to my office and set up my tape recorder to record the conversation. I assumed I would hear more information than I could remember. I dialed the international number. Once, twice, three times the phone rang. It was more of a horn sound than a ring.

"Hello," a deep voice spoke.

"I'm calling for a David Olatunde," I announced.

"Who is calling, please?" the voice asked pleasantly .

"Brian Wizard. From America."

"Brian Wizard, this is David. I am glad you called. You have responded positively to Mohammed Abacha's request. This is good. You will make many people happy, myself included. This is what I need for you to do . . ."

I was glad I was taping the call while David explained to me the business proposition. For a scam artist, this man came across as sincere as Mother Teresa. I wrote down some of the details, the most important one being the amount of money David was talking about: five hundred million U.S. dollars. To be released to me in twenty installments of twenty-five million dollars each.

David told me the source of the money. "It is looted government funds. Looted by Mohammed's father, General Sani Abacha, during his reign as Commander in Chief."

Martin walked in as I was talking. He sat quietly, allowing me to concentrate on my phone call.

David told me, "You will be allowed to keep a percentage for your effort." He then asked, "How much of a percentage would you require?"

"Whatever you think is a fair thing," I told him.

"I suggest twenty percent," David said dryly, as if no eyes should bat at a cool five million dollar commission.

"Twenty percent it is," I calmly agreed.

"I must go to Cotonou, Republic of Benin, to initiate paperwork. I need you to wire me seven hundred and twenty dollars to pay for this trip, and some up-front fees for processing this money. It is well worth your while to invest this small amount of money for such a large return," David explained.

"Well," I responded. "I'll have to think that one over. I've got a wife, and a business to consider," I lied. I was betting on the fact that this was a scam. "I'll see what I can do. I'll call you back in a few days."

David continued his sales pitch, explaining that he had already overcome many obstacles in setting up the transfer of this money. He only needed someone to send it to. The transfer had already cost him $94,000 U.S. in fees. "There are only a few more details to complete," he assured me.

He also explained that I would have to come to Cotonou to sign papers.

"Do not delay on this matter, Mr. Wizard. We need to conclude this first shipment within two weeks. Call me Monday at the latest. I will send you my home phone number by fax, and more information." David's tone of voice was authoritative. He ended with, "Do you have a fax machine?"

"Yes, I do," I told him, then gave him its number.

After hanging up, I looked at Martin. "Man, I wish this wasn't a scam. This guy just told me he has five hundred million dollars to give me in twenty-five million dollar increments."

"All for you?" Martin asked.

"I get to keep twenty percent. Five million per installment. One hundred million in total," I answered.

"Do you have to go to Africa?" Martin asked.

"Pass the atlas. He wants me to meet him in a town called Cotonou. In the Republic of Benin." Looking at the map, I saw that Benin borders Nigeria's west. "It could be a great trip," I told Martin. "Look, Cotonou is on the coast. I could use some beach time."

"Beats this damn fog," Martin concurred.

I went to the internet for a search on Benin, the republic thereof. My research turned up this travel advisory and visa requirements:

Go-Global.com
http://www.Go-Global.com

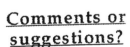
Benin

Country Description: Benin is a developing West African country. Its capital city is Porto Novo; however, the city of Cotonou is the main port and largest city; the site of the international airport and most government, commercial, and tourist activity. Tourist facilities in Cotonou are available, but are not fully developed elsewhere.

Entry Requirements: A visa is required. Travelers should obtain the latest information from the Embassy of the Republic of Benin, 2737 Cathedral Avenue, N.W., Washington, D.C. 20008, telephone (202) 232-6656. Overseas, inquiries should be made at the nearest Beninese embassy or consulate.

Medical Facilities: Medical facilities in Benin are limited. Not all medicines are available, and doctors and hospitals often expect immediate cash payment for health services. U.S. medical insurance is not always valid or accepted outside the United States. The Medicare/Medicaid program does not provide for payment of medical services outside the United States. Travelers have found supplemental medical insurance with specific overseas and medical evacuation coverage to be useful. For additional health information, travelers can contact the Centers for Disease Control and Prevention's international travelers hotline at 404) 332-4559. Internet: http://www.cdc.gov/.

Information on Crime: Street crime, especially within Cotonou, continues to rise. Most robberies and muggings occur along the Marina Boulevard and the beach near the hotels frequented by international visitors. Some of the incidents reported involve the use of force, often by armed persons, with occasional minor injury to the victim. Isolated areas are best avoided.

Business fraud stemming from Nigerian scam operations targets foreigners, including Americans, and poses a danger of financial loss and physical harm. Persons contemplating business deals in Benin with individuals promoting investment in Nigeria, especially the Central Bank of Nigeria or the Nigerian National Petroleum Company, are strongly urged to check with the U.S. Department of Commerce or the U.S. Department of State before providing any information, making financial commitments, or traveling to Benin.

The Department of State has issued a brochure for business

Page: 1

9

travelers to Nigeria; single copies are available at no charge from the Office of American Citizens Services and Crisis Management, Room 4811, Department of State, Washington, D.C. 20520-4818. Please enclose a stamped, self-addressed envelope.

The loss or theft of a U.S. passport abroad should be reported immediately to the local police and to the nearest U.S. embassy or consulate. The pamphlets "A Safe Trip Abroad" and "Tips for Travelers to Sub-Saharan Africa" provide useful information on protecting personal security while traveling abroad and on travel in the region in general. Both are available from the Superintendent of Documents, U.S. Government Printing Office, Washington, D.C. 20402.

Road Safety and In-Country Travel Conditions: Travelers should exercise caution when traveling in Benin as the roads range from fair to very poor. Travel at night, outside of population centers, poses a risk principally because of poor road conditions. There are paved roads in Cotonou, along the coast and one paved road north to Niger. Other roads are hard packed sand. All roads, paved or not, are pot-holed and narrow. Motorcycle traffic is very heavy, and trucks are usually overloaded.

Drug Penalties: U.S. citizens are subject to the laws of the country in which they are traveling. Penalties for possession, use or trafficking in illegal drugs are strict and convicted offenders can expect jail sentences and fines.

Embassy Location/Registration: U.S. citizens are encouraged to register with the U.S. Embassy in Cotonou at Rue Caporal Anani Bernard, and to obtain updated information on travel and security in Benin. The U.S. Embassy's mailing address is B.P. 2012, Cotonou, Benin. The telephone numbers are (229) 30-06-50, 30-05-13, and 30-17-92. The fax numbers are (229) 30-14-39 and 30-19-74.

Page: 2

EMBASSY OF THE REPUBLIC OF BENIN
2737 CATHEDRAL AVENUE, N.W.
WASHINGTON, D.C. 20008
TEL: (202) 232-6656
FAX: (202) 265-1996

VISA REQUIREMENTS
EFFECTIVE FEBRUARY 1993

1. Two (2) application forms in legible writing.
They can be copied if need to be.

2. Two (2) passport size photos.

3. International Certificate of Vaccination (yellow fever).

4. Visa is issued for ninety (90) days: Multiple Entry and Transit within
3 months. Extensions may be obtained at the Immigration office.

5. A $20.00 (Twenty dollars) fee for each applicant (cash, money order or
certified cheque only. No personal cheque, please).

6. A letter of guarantee from employer or travel Agency or Xerox of round trip
ticket or a Bank letter of guarantee.

- Join your passport to the forms.

- Please, allow 48 hours for issuance of visa.

- Passport must be valid for at least six (6) months and if it is to be sent
back by mail, please enclose self addressed certified envelope or an
express mail envelope.

The requirements were no problem until it came to the part about me having to have a yellow fever shot. That was not going to happen. I don't want yellow fever, starting with taking the shot. I realized I was going to have to come up with an excuse not to go.

That was enough business for a Saturday. On my way home, I decided to stop at the local pub. The pub's proprietor, Dennis, is as much the town therapist as he is the provider of spirit-laden drink. If there's something on your mind that you want to discuss, Dennis will take the time to lend you an ear, along with his advice, or at least his straightforward opinion.

Making myself comfortable at the bar, I started telling Dennis about my latest possible storyline for a novel. "I've only received two e-mails and had one phone conversation, so far. It has an interesting plot. Big money."

Dennis listened to me as he made his customary moves to set me up with my usual beer. I don't like to drink large quantities of beer, so I usually get the strong stuff. Something micro-brewed to a high specific gravity. Eight-point-one percent alcohol is nice, especially if it is an amber beer. One twelve-ounce glass of the high octane and you will experience a moment of relaxation.

"This Nigerian thing has the potential of becoming an amazing story," I told Dennis as he placed an opened bottle of 211-Steel Reserve in front of me, accompanied by a bowl of mixed nuts, "Five hundred mill is serious coinage. If it's a scam there's a story. If it's not a scam, and I receive the money, there will definitely be a story, or two.

"How much space do you think it would take to store that much money?" I asked, just before I chewed a cashew nut and took my first swig of beer.

"You can stash as much of it as you want in here," Dennis offered, with an open-armed gesture.

I spun on the barstool to estimate the room's size. Its floor was an easy forty-three hundred square feet, while the entire room was a good forty-three thousand cubic feet.

"We can't close down the only pub in town," I countered. "We'll have to put up a wall." We laughed, then I turned serious. "I'm hoping for a cashier's check."

"How'd they come up with your name?" was Dennis's next question.

"They said they found it in the Chamber of Commerce. I can only imagine they looked under G, for Greedy, with a cross reference to S, for Stupid, and there I was," I proposed.

"Greedy, stupid, and gullible is what it would take," Dennis assured me.

"Greedy and gullible," I remarked. "The Double-G Syndrome."

*   *   *

I didn't think too much about David and his need for my money until I returned to my office on the following Monday. At my noon, it was his nine in the evening. I called his office number just the same. I heard the squeal of a fax machine. "Hmmm, this could be better," I mused. I wrote him a note:

Brian Wizard
USA

David,
I suppose you are disappointed by my lack of immediate response regarding the money you need to conduct our business. Unfortunately, it will take me some time to raise the extra money.
I asked a few friends who are financially secure if they could make me a loan, but you know how that goes. A man's money is like his woman, he guards her as if she was a jewel and doesn't want to share her with anyone, not even his brother.
So, you must exercise patience, as I do what I can to raise the money you need.

                     We'll talk soon,
                     Brian Wizard

*   *   *

Almost a week had passed since my last conversation with David. I had received no new e-mails from Mo, either. Over the years, I have learned not to take business home. Otherwise, I would end up thinking about business and not about the pleasures of serenity and leisure found at my estate.

I can tell I'm researching a good story when I feel stomach butterflies fluttering inside me. All I need to do is translate my own excitement into the written word. When I opened my office door, the buzz within me tickled my sense of excitement at the sight of a rolled-up fax in front of the machine. The fluttering continued as I unrolled the paper and found the message was from David.

"Ahhh," I sighed in relief, as I read the fax. This new information was a third party confirmation that there really was an Abacha family. A family that consisted of a dead general, as well as an arrested son and wife.

The real prize was finding David's home phone number and instructions for me to call him. Unlike me, David was willing to take business home.

The time came for me to sit down, shut up, and do some serious research on the internet. I did a search using the keyword "Nigeria." A plethora of information came up. I went right for the links to the local newspapers. If the newspapers were free to print whatever they wanted, then I would have a well-rounded resource of third party opinions and reports.

The first news articles confirmed the source of the money David wanted to send to me.

Monday September 20 2:27 PM ET

U.S., Britain Offer Help Recovering Nigerian Funds

Full Coverage
Nigeria News

ABUJA, Nigeria (Reuters) - Britain joined the United States Monday in offering to help Nigeria recover missing state funds diverted and hidden by the country's former military rulers.

Nigerian officials said President Clinton had written to President Olusegun Obasanjo on September 11 pledging assistance from the Federal Bureau of Investigation in tracing money transferred to the United States.

A senior presidency official said national security adviser Aliyu Mohammed Gusau had gone to the United States in connection with the matter.

``Britain is ready to assist Nigeria in her effort to recover her stolen money,'' Rod Pullen, acting high commissioner (ambassador) for the former colonial power said during a visit to Nigeria's foreign ministry.

``That will be done only through legal channels consistent with Britain's legal provisions on such matters,'' Pullen said.

Obasanjo has also written to France, Switzerland and Belgium asking for help in the recovery of funds running into billions of dollars which went missing under late dictator Sani Abacha, the officials said.

Obasanjo's predecessor, General Abdulsalami Abubakar, recovered more than $1.0 billion from Abacha's family and cronies before stepping down in May to end 15 years of army rule in Africa's most populous nation.

 **Panafrican News Agency**

Nigeria Optimistic To Recover Stolen Wealth

September 24; 1999

NEW YORK, US (PANA) - President Olusegun Obasanjo Friday said his government's drive to recover stolen public funds and stashed away in foreign banks had received positive responses from Western leaders.

He told media representatives in New York that some of the leaders the government had written to had indicated they had located some of the stolen wealth within their respective countries.

"I am very confident we will have a satisfactory success," Obasanjo said, adding that one of these leaders had asked him, during a meeting in New York, not to hesitate to seek his country's help whenever Nigeria run into a hitch in its investigation.

The Nigerian government has reportedly received assurances from President Bill Clinton of Washington's support for the effort to recover public funds siphoned from Nigeria and kept in the US.

Addressing the UN General Assembly Thursday, Obasanjo had appealed to the international community to establish an international convention for the recovery of wealth stolen from developing countries by corrupt leaders and other nationals.

He said the stolen wealth was enough to settle the huge African external debt.

He also told New York-based Nigerians that his government expected to recover more than the 700 million US dollars that his predecessor, Gen. Abdulsalami Abubakar, had already recovered.

This site is part of <u>AFRICA NEWS ONLINE</u>.

Send your thoughts to *readers@africanews.org* for our *Readers' Forum.*
When commenting on a story, please indicate the article name and date.

Real Emporium

Page: 1

16

The next article reconfirmed Mo's arrest.

Vanguard: *Lead Story*
Why FG holds Abacha's son —*OBASANJO*
Return to Vanguard front page

By Rotimi Ajayi, Emma Ujah, *Abuja* **& Kenneth Ehigiator**

PRESIDENT Olusegun Obasanjo said, last night, that Mohammed Abacha, eldest surviving son of the late Head of State was locked up for a crime more heinous than stashing away of public funds abroad.

The President had earlier in the day pleaded with the World Bank and the International Monetary Fund (IMF) to assist Nigeria in recovering stolen funds lodged in foreign banks, while the visiting President of the World Bank, Mr. James Wolfenssohn conceded that Nigeria's friends around the world had got tired of the misrule, corruption and lack of the rule of law that characterised the military rule of the past.

President Obasanjo, speaking on his regular media dialogue on NTA declared that the arrest of Mohammed Abacha "was not unconnected with a more heinous crime than stashing away of public funds abroad."

He did not explain what that heinous crime was, but said it was a crime that "people must answer for."

He added: "They must surely answer for those crimes. No sacred cow. Whoever commits an offence must pay for such a crime."

He said the detention of Mohammed did not mean that government had thrown its human rights protection policy overboard.

"We remain committed to promoting human rights and ensuring that justice is done," he said, adding: "But thorough investigation is very important, otherwise we may be doing more harm than good."

He confirmed reports that he ordered a scrutiny of the certificates of his ministers, saying anyone found wanting would be shown the way out.

He said: "If any minister resigns before the committee submits its report, I'll sympathise with him, and organise a send-off party for him, and look for a replacement for him from his state."

He said public officers must have integrity and know that "when the game is up, it's up."

17

I then checked my e-mail, but there was no note from Mo. I hooked up my tape recorder to the phone and placed a call to David.

"David, Brian Wizard. Are you sure it's okay that I call you at your home this late at night?" I asked.

"Yes, Mr. Wizard. It is good to hear from you." David greeted me cheerfully. His vocal expression then turned sad. "Terrible things have happened to our friend Mohammed. Did you receive my fax?"

"I did."

"We must move even faster now to transfer the first installment into your account. When can you come to Cotonou?"

My foremost fear of going to Cotonou was the yellow fever shot. I wanted to discourage this line of thought on David's part. "I called the Benin Embassy. They said it would take two weeks to get my visa. That being the case, I would have to guess in about a month."

"That is too long. You must get here sooner. Too much money is at stake. Do not fail us now," he warned.

"We have a bigger problem than that," I began to lie. "My woman says she'll leave me if I follow through with your request. To prove her point she didn't come home last night. We argued about me sending you money. So, there is more at stake than just money. Plus, what about my business? I can't just walk away. What about my employees?"

There was no wife, no employees, but David had to figure them all into the fictitious equation.

"Call me as soon as you can to tell me when you can come to Cotonou. Meanwhile, I need for you to do this one thing for us all now. Do not delay. Send me the money I requested so that I can go to Cotonou and finish the paperwork. Can you wire me one thousand dollars today?"

"Not today. The Western Union is sixty miles away. I only go there once a month. Perhaps next week. Okay?" I could feel my lower lip draw across my teeth. A sign of apprehension.

"Why are you always giving excuses?" David asked me in a very stern tone. "Do you want to assist us, or not?"

"Yes, I do. But it has to be comfortable for me. I can't go running off to send money to people in Africa. Not without my woman finding out. I don't want to lose her. Plus, she owns half of the business. You understand all that, don't you, David?" I knew I could win some ground in this argument. I just had to fight for it.   18

"I tell my woman nothing about my business, Mr. Wizard. You should do the same," David advised. "Do what you can and call me when you are ready to send money. If I can, I will find a way to borrow more money. You will need to come to Cotonou soon."

I learned from that experience that Mr. Seemingly-Pleasant David the Nigerian had a hard side to him.

The thought struck me that perhaps there was something on the internet about Nigerian scams. My search came up with more than I could imagine.

Nigeria - The 419 Coalition Website

We Fight the Nigerian Scam.

The Nigerian Scam Defined

A Five Billion US$ (to date) worldwide Scam which has run for the last Fourteen Years under Successive Governments of Nigeria. It is also referred to as "Advance Fee Fraud", "419 Fraud" (Four-One-Nine) after the relevant section of the Criminal Code of Nigeria, "The Fax Scam" and "The Nigerian Connection" (mostly in Europe). However, it is usually called plain old "419" even by the Nigerians themselves.

The Scam operates as follows: the target receives an unsolicited fax or letter from Nigeria containing either a money laundering or other illegal proposal **OR you may receive a Legal and Legitimate business proposal by normal means.** Common variations on the Scam include "overinvoiced" or "double invoiced" oil or other supply and service contracts where your Bad Guys want to get the overage out of Nigeria; crude oil and other commodity deals; a "bequest" left you in a will; and "money cleaning" where your Bad Guy has a lot of currency that needs to be "chemically cleaned" before it can be used and he needs the cost of the chemicals. Or the victim will just be stiffed on a legitimate goods or services contract...the variations are very creative and virtually endless.

At some point, the victim is asked to pay up front an Advance Fee of some sort, be it an "Advance Fee", "Transfer Tax", "Performance Bond", or to extend credit, grant COD privileges, whatever. If the victim pays the Fee, there are many "Complications" which require still more advance payments until the victim either quits, runs out of money, or both. If the victim extends credit etc. he may also pay such fees ("nerfund" etc.), and then he is stiffed with NO Effective Recourse.

The Nigerian Scam is, according to published reports, the Third largest industry in Nigeria. Our research demonstrates rather conclusively that, in effect, **successive Governments of Nigeria ARE the Scammers** - therefore, victims have little recourse in this matter, and **monies stolen by 419 operations are almost Never Recovered from Nigeria.**

Please **review the 419 Coalition Inquiry and Information links which follow below on this page.** The email address of 419 Coalition is alphae@rica.net and Snailmail is The 419 Coalition, Twin Maples, 3891 North Valley Pike, Harrisonburg, VA, 22802, USA. **Freewill non-tax deductible contributions are always appreciated.**

And if YOU Have Received a Nigerian Scam/419 Letter Please Be Sure to Scroll Down and READ the What Do If You Receive a Nigerian Scam/419 Letter Section BELOW.

THE FIVE RULES FOR DOING BUSINESS WITH NIGERIA

Courtesy of The 419 Coalition

1. NEVER pay anything up front for ANY reason.
2. NEVER extend credit for ANY reason.
3. NEVER do ANYTHING until their check clears.
4. NEVER expect ANY help from the Nigerian Government.
5. NEVER rely on YOUR Government to bail you out.

What To Do If You Receive A Nigerian Scam/419 Letter

United States Citizens and Residents

1. If you are a United States Citizen or Resident and have suffered NO Financial Loss, write "No Financial Loss - For Your Database" on the documents you received and Fax them to the US Secret Service Task Force handling Scam matters at 202-406-6930. Actual hardcopy of the Bad Guy document(s) is required to add your Bad Guy information to the Task Force Database for legal reasons, merely telling Task Force about it will NOT suffice.

You may also email the 419er documents, especially any Banking Data they may have given you, marked as described above, to Task Force Main in DC; that is also acceptable.

Since Task Force is Very Busy dealing with cases in which there Have been financial losses, it is NOT customary for them to contact you in cases where there has been No loss. But it is Very Important that you get your Bad Guy data into the Task Force Database, so DO send it along.

2. IF you are a United States Citizen or Resident and YOU HAVE SUFFERED A FINANCIAL LOSS write "Financial Loss - Contact Me ASAP" on the documents you have received and Fax them to the Task Force at 202-406-6930 and give Your

20

telephone number(s). A Secret Service Agent will call you back as soon as possible to discuss the matter with you (don't worry, you're Not in any trouble). You may also email the 419er materials, especially any Banking Data they have given you, to <u>Task Force Main in DC</u> marked as described above.

If you don't get a callback soon enough to suit you, call the **Task Force Voice at 202-406-5850** and tell the Operator (or voicemail) that it's Urgent, you want to talk to an Agent as soon as possible, and give your name and telephone number(s).

International Citizens and Residents

1. **If you are Not a US Citizen or Resident, but there is ANY US CONNECTION to your Case at all**, follow the instructions for US Citizens and Residents given above, and be Sure to include any US banking data on your Bad Guys if you have any.

Clearly State what the US Connection is, and provide backup material to support the US Connection. Also notify your own Nation's authorities as in #2 below.

International and Your Case has NO US Connection:

2. Notify your Own Nation's National Law Enforcement Agency and your Own Nation's Foreign Office.

3. Please **Fax hardcopy** of your Bad Guy Data correspondence you received to the US Task Force at **202-406-6930, especially any banking data**, so that they can be included in the Task Force Database, state what Country you are sending from, and state whether there has been a Loss or there is No Loss. **You can also email the material to <u>Task Force Main in DC</u>** marked as described above.

In cases without a direct US connection it is unlikely that Task Force will contact you, however, **there IS an an informal group of National and International Law Enforcement Agencies which meets and shares Information and Data on Nigerian Scam operations, and it is Important that your Bad Guy data be on record to be included in these discussions.**

Therefore, whether or not your case has a US connection, **do not fail** to Fax your Bad Guy data, especially banking data, to Task Force, properly annotated with Your Country, Loss or No Loss etc., at 202-406-6930 **in addition** to reporting your case to your National authorities as described above. And remember you can also email your 419er documents to **<u>Task Force Main in DC</u>** as you wish.

For Everybody Everywhere

1. **If you have NOT suffered a financial loss, so the matter is not Urgent, you may alternatively SNAILMAIL the Scam documents you have received to the United States Secret Service, Financial Crimes Division, 419 Task Force, 950 H Street, Washington, DC, 20001-4518, USA. But be sure to mark your documents "No Financial Loss - For Your Database" as described above.**

2. If you wish, file a Complaint with the Nigerian Embassy in your Nation. Won't help much, but can't hurt much. The fax number of the Nigerian Ambassador in DC is 202-775-7385 and the fax number of the Nigerian Ambassador to the United Nations is 212-697-1970 (until they change them that is). The voice numbers of the Embassy of Nigeria in DC are 202-986-8400 & 202-822-1500; the fax number there is 202-775-1385. The mailing addresses of the Embassy of Nigeria in DC are: Embassy of Nigeria, 1333 16th St., N.W., Washington, D.C., 20036 and also Embassy of Nigeria, 2201 M. Street, N.W., Washington, D.C., 20037.

3. If you decide to fax Your Nigerian Scammers and tell them off, be sure and tell them 419 Coalition sent you - we LIKE for them to know Who's Sticking It To Them.

Canada - Country Specific Instructions - Canada

Although there is a 419 investigative team of the RCMP based in Ottawa, this is NOT where citizens should direct complaints or inquiries. Regional Offices of the RCMP Commercial Crime Branch are the appropriate places to direct inquiries or data. The phone/fax numbers of the nearest CCB office are available from Any detachment of the RCMP/GRC. Data forwarded to the Regional CCB office is used to establish regional statistics and will be sent to the Central Team.

And please do fax hardcopy of your Bad Guy Data, especially Nigerian Scammer Banking Data to the US Task Force, appropriately marked with Canada, Loss (or No Loss as the Case May Be), No US Connection, For Your Database, at 202-406-6930. You may also email such data to **Task Force Main in DC** if you prefer.

If there IS a US Connection, please Follow These Instructions for Canada **AND ALSO** follow the instructions for US Citizens and Residents given above.

You may also access the **Royal Canadian Mounted Police Website (RCMP/GRC)** which contains a section on the Nigerian Scam.

South Africa - Country Specific Instructions - South Africa

Please contact Captain SC Schambriel of Commercial Crime, Head Office, at telephone number (012) 339 1203 or preferably **fax** the information to him at (012) 339 1202.

Also please fax the Scam documents, especially Nigerian Scammer banking data, to the US Task Force at 202-406-6930 appropriately marked South Africa - Loss (or No Loss as the case may be) - For Your Database. Please be SURE to state if there is any US Connection to your 419ers' operations, Particularly if there is US Banking Data on them. You may also email such relevant data to **Task Force Main in DC** if you prefer to do it that way.

The **South African Police Service** maintains a **419 Scams/Nigerian Letters Alert** on their website.

Nigerian Scam News, Links, Information, & Analysis

Additional Data and Analysis on the Nigerian Scam, plus LATEST NEWS and Other Information follows. PLEASE READ EVERY PAGE to get a Comprehensive View of the Nigerian Scam and the Efforts of Public and Private Agencies to Combat It - No Fluff Here! LINKS to other Scam Fighting Websites are also provided below for your convenience.

- 419 COALITION LATEST NEWS ON NIGERIAN SCAM/419 OPERATIONS
- 419 COALITION 1999 NEWS ON NIGERIAN SCAM/419 OPERATIONS
- 419 COALITION 1998 NEWS ON NIGERIAN SCAM/419 OPERATIONS
- 419 COALITION 1997 NEWS ON NIGERIAN SCAM/419 OPERATIONS
- 419 COALITION 1996 NEWS ON NIGERIAN SCAM/419 OPERATIONS

- Press Release by Congressman Ed Markey of Massachusetts on the Nigerian Advanced Fee Fraud Prevention Act of 1998
- Introduction by Congressman Ed Markey of Massachusetts to the Nigerian Advanced Fee Fraud Prevention Act of 1998
- Full Text of H.R. 3916: the "Nigerian Advanced Fee Fraud Prevention Act of 1998"

- US Department of State - Bureau of International Narcotics and Law Enforcement Affairs - Publication 10465 - "Nigerian Advance Fee Fraud" (Adobe Acrobat Reader Required. This is a pdf file of about 1 gig - a Long load but worth it)
- US Department of State - Tips for Business Travelers to Nigeria
- US Department of State - Travel Warning on Nigeria
- US Secret Service Home Page - Click on "Investigations" for Warning and Advisory on Nigerian Scam - 419 - Advance Fee Fraud
- US Secret Service Nigerian Scam Warning in Various Languages - The English version is on the Secret Service site menued above

- Sample Nigerian Scam/419 Letters
- Government of Nigeria Involvement in the Scam
- Government of Nigeria Media Campaigns
- 419 Coalition Recommendations on the Nigerian Scam
- Select Nigerian Organizations Fighting the Nigerian Scam
- Response to Nigerian Gov't Statement on IIS & 419 Coalition
- Alpha Electronics Statement on the Nigerian Scam
- 419 Coalition Peace with Honor Proposal (Expired 31 MAR 97)
- 419 Coalition at YOUR site
- About The 419 Coalition

LINKS TO SITES FIGHTING THE NIGERIAN SCAM HERE!!

Most in English, but also some in French, Spanish, German, Dutch, & Indonesian/Malay languages.

Please Read the ENTIRE site BEFORE contacting 419 Coalition for information, questions etc., as ALL AVAILABLE INFORMATION AND DATA IS ALREADY SUMMARIZED AND POSTED UP ON THIS SITE. Pay particular attention to the What To Do If You Receive a Nigerian Scam Letter data above, and menu items Latest News, 1996 News, Government of Nigeria Involvement in the Scam, and GOV of Nigeria Media Campaigns. The odds are that whatever you want to know is already posted up here for you to read - Look First - THEN contact us if what you want to know is not already covered. Remember - Read First - Then Inquire.

419 Coalition also respectfully asks **Journalists** to do the same. We at 419 Coalition **Appreciate Immensely the contributions of Journalists in reporting on the Nigerian Scam** as publicity is one of the Very Best Ways to educate the public and thereby increase the operational costs of the 419ers, reducing their net margin.

However, we average 60 "front door" hits a day on this site, every day, seven days a week, we are very busy, and going over material which is Already posted up is understandably very time consuming. So please, **Read First THEN contact us as required**. Also, to facilitate matters for you in your reporting, please note that the Coordinator of 419 Coalition is personally responsible for every word up on this 419 Coalition website, and you have permission up front to quote him directly, in context, on all data and analysis you find on this site.

All who wish to do so may also check the site of our companion Organization, **International Investigation Services**, for additional information on the Nigerian Scam as required.

You are also urged to review the Nigerian Scam/419 Advisory on the US Secret Service Website. Click on "Investigations" after you get to the Site and the Advance Fee Fraud/419 Advisory will be a menu item.

In general, 419 Coalition does NOT need to see copies of your Scam letters unless they contain something unique, but you MUST send them to Task Force as described in the What To Do section. If your 419 Letter DOES contain something unique, please do smailmail it, email it, or fax it to 419 Coalition at 540-434-7561.

Please Note that all information, inquiries, and data furnished to 419 Coalition are considered a matter of Public Record which 419 Coalition reserves the right to use, act on, disseminate, or refer to appropriate Governments, agencies, authorities, or organizations as we, in our sole judgement, see fit.

When there is nothing you can do about a situation, then it is best to sit back and see what happens on its own. While waiting, I tried to figure out how I could make this scam work to my benefit without it costing me any money. I decided to contact Mo. What could I say that might prompt him to spill some beans? I had questions. For example, how did a prison inmate have e-mail access? I also wondered if I could get Mo, or whomever this pen-pal might be, to open up on a personal level. Maybe get beyond the scam.

```
        To: "mohameduz abacha" <mohameduz@mailcity.com>
      From: Brian Wizard <bwizard@pop3.eoni.com>
   Subject: Re: ALLOCATION.
        Cc:
       Bcc:
X-Attachments:
```

Mohameduz,

Today I go on a business trip in an attempt to raise some money. Of course, I have a stack of bills that I need to attend to first. We can only hope that the art buyers are in the mood for some Brian Wizard artwork. Don't lose faith, all good things come to pass, and the darkest hours of the night are just before the dawn.

Your position must be hard and all consuming. Again, I invite you to write to me and let out some of your frustrations via e-mail. I am a minister and I do listen well. Talking about your life and situation may not seem like much, but if you let go of your problems through talk then some of the pressure within you will lessen. We all need a shoulder to cry on, an ear to listen, and a heart, even that of a stranger, to lend compassion. Those are things money can't buy. These are things one man gives to another for free.

There is the old saying, "A man who builds a bridge without a sound structual plan is a man about to get wet." The things we do in life are like the building of bridges. From one side of the river of life to the other we criss cross the ravine in search of the ultimate passage.

Sometimes we traverse the raging waters without getting wet, other times we all but drown, and then, well . . . it happens, we drown. That is why it is good to travel with friends, just in case we are swept away in the rapids. True friends will risk all they have to save you from peril, even if you have rushed into the water foolishly, not looking at the river for what it really is: unmerciful, unrelenting and undaunting to a man's mortal efforts to survive the ride.

Even though the river of life can't be tamed, it can be negotiated successfully. On its banks are the forests, the plains, the ample supply of life giving foods, shelter and medicine.

I am negotiating the waters with you, my friend. Paddling against the current as best I can. Keeping us on course and out of the rapids. Still, I'm just a man in the big river. My stature is small in comparison, yet I fight the rapids, the currents, the falls as best I can to make my journey toward success. If I end up being a poor choice of paddleman then my only excuse is: the river won. It may win my body, my life, but it can never take away from me the history of my efforts to succeed in navigating the ruthless waterway.

In the end, we work hard to be able to say, "I paddled as best I could." It is best to say that downstream, when the water is calm and the current is mellow, and we are resting upon the sandy shore, drenched in the warmth of the sun, as we fill our bellies with the fruits of the earth, and of course, sharing the good fortune with everyone we can.

SO, I'll be out of touch for a few days, working on negotiating the river of life through the whitewater rapids I have come across. Hold on, my friend, the calm waters lie just ahead . . . if the river doesn't claim us.

                          Talk to me,
                              Brian Wizard

http://www.brianwizard.com

* * *

I was happy to read some personal details about Mo, and his willingness to tell some stories, as noted in his next e-mail:

---

mohameduz abacha,10/2/99 9:57 AM -0700,Re: RE; ALLOCATION.

```
X-From_: mohameduz@mailcity.com  Sat Oct  2 09:57:47 1999
To: bwizard@eoni.com
Date: Sat, 02 Oct 1999 16:57:02  0000
From: "mohameduz abacha" <mohameduz@mailcity.com>
Mime-Version: 1.0
X-Sent-Mail: off
Subject: Re: RE; ALLOCATION.
X-Sender-Ip: 208.243.226.224
Organization: MailCity  (http://www.mailcity.lycos.com:80)


        BRIAN WIZARD I HAVE A LOT OF PROBLEMS ARREST NEARLY EVERY OTHER WEEK  DAVID WILL TELL YOU
OF WHAT HAPPENED TO ME LAST WEEK HE WAS THERE FOR MY ASSISTANCE NO OTHER PERSON. I PRAY THIS FIRST
PART TRANSFER SHOULD BE CONCLUDED THIS WEEK DAVID IS BACK TO LAGOS CALL HIM.

    I HAVE A LOT OF STORIES TO TELL THAT SHOULD WHEN WE ALL MEET.

    I AM MARRIED. MANY CALL ME MO. THIS IS NOT BAD

    I EXPECT YOUR RESPONSE, AGIAN
    I AM 47YEARS OLD.
    BE BLESS.
```

As he stated, now was not the time to tell stories. When we do meet there would be time to tell tall tales of the scam. I suppose he had to draw a line of familiarity somewhere in the electronic sand. After all, familiarity breeds contempt. Being the son of a military dictator would teach that on a regular daily basis.

I checked the Nigerian News Network for anything of interest. I found this:

Vanguard: Newsreel
Abacha's son, Mustapha, 'Rogers' in Lagos court today ...*May be tried under Section 316 of Criminal Code*

Return to Vanguard front page

IF the Chief Security Officer (CSO) to the late General Sani Abacha, Major Hamza Al-Mustapha, eldest son of the late head of state, Mohammed and security guard Sgt. Rogers Msheila are charged with murder in Lagos today they are likely to be tried under Section 316 of the criminal code law of Lagos State.

Section 316 says "A person who unlawfully kills another under any of the following circumstances i.e. to say (I) if the offender intends to cause the death of the person killed, or that of some other persons.

(ii) If the offender intends to do to the person killed or some other persons some grievous harm.

(iii) If the death is caused by means of an act done in the prosecution of an unlawful purpose which act is of such nature as to be likely to endanger human life.

(iv) If the offender intends to do grievous harm to some persons but the purpose of facilitating the commission of an offence which is such that such an offender may be arrested without warrant, or for the purpose of facilitating the flight of an offender who has committed or attempted to commit such an offence.

(v) If death is caused by administering any stupifying or any overpowering thing for either of the purposes last aforesaid.

(vi) If death is caused by willfully stopping the breath of any person for either of such purposes is guilty of murder.

In the second case it is immaterial that the offender did not intend to hurt the particular person killed.

In the third case it is immaterial that the offender did not intend to hurt anybody. In the last three cases it is immaterial that the offender did not intend to cause death or did not know that death was likely to result.

Section 319 (1) says anybody that commits such offence faces death penalty.

Back to top

Vanguard Transmitted Wednesday, 13 October, 1999

* * *

The next time I checked my e-mail I found this note from Mo, as if he knew I had been reading the Nigerian Newspapers:

```
X-From_: mohameduz@mailcity.com  Mon Oct 18 20:04:52 1999
To: bwizard@eoni.com
Date: Tue, 19 Oct 1999 03:03:33  0000
From: "mohameduz abacha" <mohameduz@mailcity.com>
```

ATTN; BRIAN WIZARD
        I WONDER WHY YOU FAIL TO CALL DAVID OR COMMUNICATE WITH ME ON THE NET KNOWING FULLY WELL ABOUT MY TRIAL, MAY BE WHAT YOU HAD ABOUT THE MURDER AND RAPE CASE.
        I NEVER MURDERED OR RAPE ANY BODY,I WAS ONLY ROPED INTO THE CASE,SINCE GOVERNMENT CAN NOT LAY HANDS ON ANY CHARGE AGAINST ME. TAKE WHAT I HAVE TOLD YOU.
        DAVID LEFT FOR BENIN TO-DAY 18-10-99 WITH MY BROTHER IN-LAW WHO WILL WITHNESS THE WHOLE TRANSACTION.HIS NAME IS [PRINCE UZOMA MADU].>ITS WITH THIS NAME THEY ARE GOING TO LODGE IN THE HOTEL.
        THEY ARE STAYING IN EITHE R IN VIN-KIL-FIN HOTEL ON TELL NO; 229-313814 OR IN HOTEL DE L'ETOILE ON TELL; 229-30264 1 OR 229-303842.ASK OF PRINCE UZOMA MADU AND YOU WILL BE GIVEN THIER ROOM NO.
        ONE GOOD THING IS THAT DAVID WENT WITH THE DIPLOMATIC CHANNEL DIRECTOR MR SUNNY ALIBA WHO WILL ASSIST HIM.

                        REGARDS
                        M.ABACHA

I hadn't called David for two reasons: 1. It was very expensive. 2. What did I have to say to make him understand that I didn't want to go to Benin? If I was such a key element in the transfer of this money, why would I have to do anything but stay here and receive the loot?

I called David at the hotel in Benin.

"I'm calling for Prince Uzoma Madu," I reported to the French-speaking person who answered the phone. I believe he said something to the effect of, "Please hold." African drum music filled my ear. It was an interesting version of elevator music.

"Hello," David's familiar voice said.

"David, Brian Wizard. What's up?"

"Mr. Wizard, it is good that you have called me. I have arranged for the security company that holds the first installment to fax to you documents they have prepared in your name. Keep these documents confidential and in a safe place. You will need them when you arrive in Cotonou."

"How long will you be at this number?" I asked.

"I will be home tomorrow. Call me after you receive the documents," David instructed.

"Okay. I'll try."

It was comforting to know that David didn't need my money after all. Maybe he was going to do everything he could on that end, without my financial assistance. That would be great. Then the bad news came.

"Before they can send the documents, you must pay them five hundred dollars. You must send this money today. Wire the money by Western Union to Frank Uwen." David spelled the last name for me.

"That's a lot of money, David," I stated, while wondering who Frank Uwen was.

"Mr. Wizard. You are an American. You have such money," David told me, as if he were familiar with my bank statement. "Do not fail us now. These documents will prove to you that what I am telling you is the truth. Call me as soon as you have the confirmation numbers for the Western Union wire."

"It will be late, your time," I warned him.

"The front desk will take your message and bring it to me. Please, do not fail," David begged.

Oh boy, the pressure was on. David was such a salesman. Well, what the hell. I had already allocated a four thousand dollar budget for this research. I was curious about what documents could assure me David was not a scam artist. Before I sent any money, I decided to contact Western Union, and ask:

```
Hello,
        I have been asked to help a friend in Benin, a West African nation, by
sending him $720 via Western Union. This is a sort of weird, and I fear it might be a scam. So, I am
asking you if you can do a quick search on a computer and see if you turn up an unusual amount of
American tranfers to Frank Uwen in Benin. I'd like to know ASAP, for if this is a scam, I'd like to
break it. I'd appreciate your assistance. Thanks.
        Brian Wizard
```

It didn't take Western Union long to reply.

Sue_Feeney%WESTERNUNION@westernunion.com,9/23/99 3:11 PM +0100,Re:Ben

```
X-From_: Sue_Feeney%WESTERNUNION@westernunion.com  Thu Sep 23 08:12:45 1999
From: Sue_Feeney%WESTERNUNION@westernunion.com
Subject: Re:Benin money transfer

Because of security issues, I cannot tell you how many Money Transfers
Frank Uwen has received.  I did check with our Security Department and his
name is not listed in our Scam Log.  We always caution our customers about
sending money to someone they don't know.  If you are in the U.S. and you
decide to go ahead and send the $750, I would recommend sending it by
credit card, as you can then dispute the charges with your credit card
company if there is a problem.  To send by MasterCard, Visa or Discover,
you can call 1-800-CALL-CASH.
```

Foolishly, I know, I sent the money. Every story has to have a research and development budget. I could only hope the documents were an investment that would pay off. I compromised David's request for a thousand dollars and only sent him his original request for seven hundred and twenty dollars.

I called David and gave him the confirmation number. He sounded very relieved that he had taken some money from me. Ironically, I felt like the fish on the hook.

*   *   *

It took two days of suspense before the documents from Koffie M. Biyah, Director of Trans-World Security Company, arrived via the fax machine. They were almost worth their weight in gold as trophies to hang on the wall. Well, three out of the four were. The first document, the opening letter, clearly stated that I was requested to arrive in Cotonou with thirty-five hundred dollars. That did not make me feel as if I had got my money's worth. The other three, though, were classic pieces of scam material.

I loved the *Certificate of Ownership* of two galvanized boxes containing twenty-five million dollars worth of U.S. hundred dollar bills.

Everything about the approved dispatch for the money from the *Diplomatic Channel Centre* looked good.

The *National Drug Law Enforcement Agency's Clearance Certificate* for the money was nothing short of a Get-Out-Of-Jail-Free card.

TRANS -WORLD SECURITY COMPANY

COTONOU - REPUBLIQUE DU BENIN
AVENUE JEAN PAUL II
03 BP : 25347 Recette Principale
TEL/FAX 229 – 33 – 70 – 56

COTONOU, 29TH SEPTEMBER 1999

TEL/FAX : 229 - 33 – 70 - 56

ATTN :   MR. BRIAN WIZARD
P. O. BOX 2,
WALLOWA, OR 97885
U.S.A.

Dear Sir,

COPY OF CERTIFICATE OF OWNERSHIP IS HEREBY SENT TO YOU INDICATING YOUR FUND UNDER OUR CUSTODY AND COVERING THIS FUND. PLEASE SIGN THE BENEFICIARY COLUMN AND RETURN SAME BY FAX TO THIS OFFICE FOR RECORD PURPOSE.

COULD YOU PLEASE COME FORWARD WITHIN TWO WEEK FROM TODAY, WITH THE SUM REPRESENTING THE TELEGRAPHIC TRANSFER CLEARANCE CERTIFICATE FOR THE MINISTRY OF FINANCE, COTONOU, REPUBLIC OF BENIN. YOU WILL BE REQUIRED TO PAY FOR THIS **T.T.C.C.** BEFORE THE BANK IN COTONOU WILL ACCEPT TO RECEIVE THE MONEY FOR WIRE TRANSFER ACCORDING TO THE MONETARY LAWS OF THIS COUNTRY.

I ADVICE THAT ON YOUR ARRIVAL IN COTONOU YOU ARE REQUIRED TO OPEN A FOREIGN DOMICILIARY ACCOUNT WITH ONE OF OUR INTERNATIONAL BANKS THROUGH WHICH YOU CAN TRANSFER YOUR FUNDS.

YOU ARE THEREFORE TO COME ALONG WITH FOUR PASSPORT SIZE PHOTO AND THE SUM OF **$3,500** FOR THIS PURPOSE.

THANKS.

-B. ANJORIN
(Accountant).

KOFFI M. BIYAH
(Director).

TRANSWORLD SECURITY

COMPANY

COTONOU - REPUBLIC OF BENIN
RUE DU CARREFOUR
03 BP : 0857 RECETTE DE JERICHO
TEL/FAX 229 – 33 – 70 – 56

CERT. N° 0986

MR. BRIAN WIZARD
P. O. BOX 2,
WALLOWA, OR. 97885,
U.S.A.

CERTIFICATE OF OWNERSHIP
****

WE, THE MANAGEMENT OF THE ABOVE SECURITY COMPANY,
HEREBY CONFIRM HAVING AS AT PRESENT UNDER OUR CUSTODY TWO
GALVANISED BOXES CONTAINING U.S DOLLAR BILLS OF $100
DENOMINATION VALUED AT **TWENTY FIVE MILLION U.S.DOLLARS
(U.S.$25M)** BEING CONSIGNMENT ON CASH ROOTING N° 9902244/
AZ000963 FROM NIGERIA.

G/BOX 1 :   FIFTEEN MILLION U.S. DOLLARS (U.S.$15 M)

G/BOX 2 :   TEN MILLION U.S.DOLLARS (U.S.$10M)

TOTAL VALUE : TWENTY FIVE MILLION U.S. DOLLARS(U.S.$25 M)

BONAFIDE OWNER
MR. BRIAN WIZARD
P. O. BOX 2,
WALLOWA, OR. 97885,
U.S.A.

SECURITY & GENERAL CHARGES
TO BE PAID BEFORE G/BOXES IS DELIVERED TO OWNER/BANK

DATED THIS ......*21st*......... DAY OF ......*September*...... 199*9*......

BENEFICIARY
MR BRIAN WIZARD

DIPLOMATIC CHANNEL CENTRE
EXTERNAL AFFAIRS BUILDING
LAGOS NIGERIA

OUR REF: DCCLN/RVDA/FOREX-09-99

YOUR REF: NG-99　　　　　　　　　　DATE: 17TH SEPTEMBER, 1999

0425503995
28770 NG.
BNP 550822B
TWSC 6151B

FROM DIPLOMATIC CHANNEL CENTRE LAGOS - NIGERIA

TO: WEST AFRICAN CLEARING HOUSE W.A.C.H

LOCAL AGENCY: TRANSWORLD SECURITIES COMPANY BENIN (CONTONOU)

TO: MR. BRIAN WIZARD

TRANSFER CASH CODE 30004 MBX 5110

MTB200/US$25M

LOCAL TRANSMITTING FUNT PRM 90

BASIC HEADER CASH FUND TRANSFER CONFIRMATION

APPLICATION HEADER: SOLDEST XXX990124 DAVID OLATUNDE

UA 200/99 SEPT/BEN TW

CASH TRANSFER FOR SETTLEMENT, DIRECT CREDIT TO ACCT. OF

BENEFICIARY: BRIAN WIZARD　　　　　IN COTONOU REPUBLIC OF BENIN.

USER HEADER PRIORITY: PACIFIC BANK ROOTING THROUGH DIPLOMATIC

CHANNEL CENTRE LAGOS NIGERIA. MP USER REFERENCE CPS 01-004/96

NARRATIVE: PLEASE RELEASE FUND TO BENEFICIARY MR.BRIAN WIZARD

UPON PERSONAL REPRESENTATION IF MATTERS ARE NORMALISED.

CASH ROOTING NO. 990224/AZ000963

copy-notice Pge 33

CURRENCY US$　　AMOUNT: US$25M.

ORDERING CUSTOMER: PACIFIC INT. MERCHANT BANK

BENEFITING CUSTOMER/ORDER: MR.BRIAN WIZARD

RECORD INFORMATION: ADVICE THE BENEFICIARY PLEASE. 'MR. BRAIN

WIZARD, U.S.A THE TRANSFER FEE OF US$54,000 PAID.

BEST REGARDS.

MR. H. TOSIN

PAY TO WIZARD

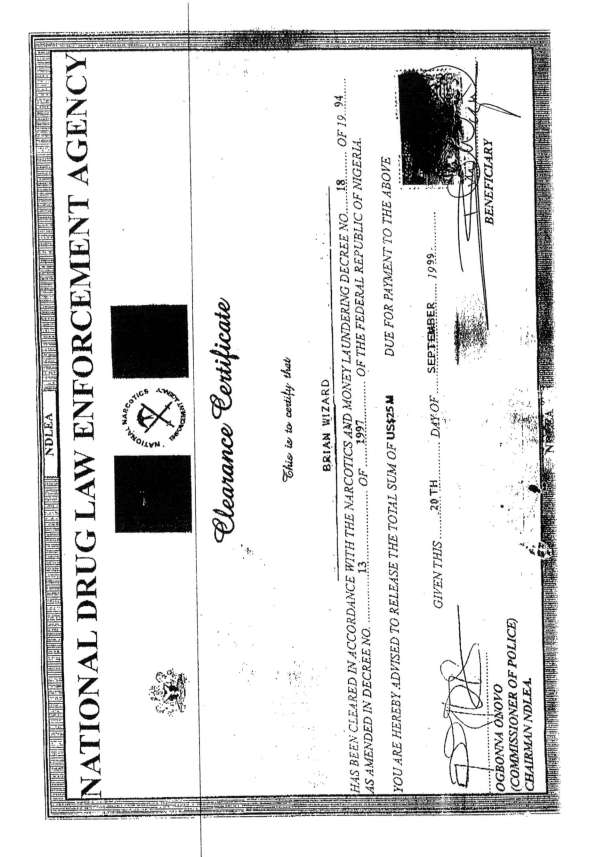

Yep, these scam souvenirs were suitable for framing, with signatures, stamps, and seals that cried, "Official!" They were about as official as any faxed copy of phony documents.

There still remained the next important question: How to be excused from going to Benin?

I called my friend, Dr. Robinson. "Doc, I need your help."

"No. I can't write you a prescription for pot," he adamantly stated, again.

"I need you to write me a note saying that I can't travel to far-away places."

"I thought you liked to travel," he remarked.

"I do, but not to every place in the world. Such as the Republic of Benin in West Africa. They have a yellow fever shot requirement for a visa."

"So, don't go."

"My presence is being requested," I explained.

"By whom?"

"By a bunch of international scamsters. Ever hear of the Nigerian 419 Scam?"

"Actually, I have," Doc reported. "I received a letter from some po-dunk African country telling me they had a few million extra dollars they wanted me to launder. Something like that."

"Those are the guys," I enthusiastically confirmed.

"Working on a new novel?" he asked.

"We're on the same page, Doc."

"You do like to take risks, don't you?"

"That's what makes me such a fun guy, and I'm not talking mushrooms, either," I kidded.

"Can you come by around five?" Doc asked.

"I'll be there."

I met with my doctor as planned. He provided my requested note. "What makes you want to deal with these gangsters, anyhow?"

Knowing him as well as I do, I brought along the paperwork David and his friends had sent me, as well as the newspaper articles. While Doc looked over the papers, I said, "Scamsters, like terrorists, only have a job if their intended victims are uninformed, or afraid. My goal is to water down their market through my entertaining investigative report. When I

35

am done with this mission, it will be 'Game Over!' for the great Nigerian 419 Scam."

"You could be biting off more than you can chew," Doc warned. "I won't be there to patch you up like before."

Doc and I go way back. He has sewn up a few lacerations, set a couple of bones, and even assisted in removing one of my testicles.

"You know my number one rule of engagement." Doc joined me in unison. We recited a frequently used code of combat I learned in Viet Nam. "Do not fire until you are fired upon, then fire for effect."

*   *   *

Excited about what the Nigerians might have up their sleeves brought me to town early the next morning. I wanted to send the note from my doctor to Trans-World Security head, Koffie Biyah, and gain his permission to bypass the need for me to travel to Benin. I decided to back up this ploy by giving David power of attorney, enabling him to act as my personal representative. Before I did anything, though, I checked my e-mail.

There was a short note from Mo that said, "*Call David now. He is at home.*" Mo's continued e-mail access re-enforced my conviction that this was just a scam.

With the tape recorder on, I placed my call. "David, Brian Wizard."

David's voice sounded groggy when he said, "Who is calling?"

"Brian Wizard. I have a note from Mo telling me to call you."

"Yes, Mr. Wizard. Did you receive the documents from Cotonou?"

"Yes. I did. Very impressive."

"You see now that I am not lying to you," David attempted to make his case.

I thought to myself, faxed copies of bogus documents don't hold up in court. I then said to David, "So, everything is in place, correct?"

"Almost," David replied.

I thought, here comes another request for money. I broke in before he could say much more.

"David, here's what I need for you to understand, and for you to do for me." I used my own stern tone of voice to mimic the way David always delivered his requests.

36

David was silent, and I continued, "I can't travel to Cotonou. My doctor does not advise it. I have a respiratory ailment that prevents me from travel by any means of transport that uses recycled air. Especially airplanes or ships."

The problem with telephone conversations and the like is that there is no body language to interpret. I could only imagine David's body language trying hard to butt in, but I wouldn't let him. After all, this call was on my dime. Dime, hell! A wad of dollar bills.

"What I am going to do is draft up a power of attorney in your name. You will be able to sign all the papers in Cotonou as my legal representative. This power of attorney will be a legal document and duly recorded in a court of law," I explained.

"You must be present in Cotonou," David insisted.

"Not necessarily true, my friend," I countered. "So pack your bags and head back across the border. Now, what did you want to tell me?"

"Before the money can be released from the security company, we must obtain a Clearance/Assessment Form. This form is called a CO_2," David explained.

"Okay," I said cheerfully. "Go get it. You're the man in charge of such things, especially after you receive the power of attorney."

"This document costs fifteen hundred dollars, U.S. I do not have any more money, nor do I know anyone else to borrow such money from," David complained. His voice expressed a real sense of worry. I was impressed by his acting skills.

"Fifteen hundred!" I exclaimed. "I thought you said you had all the forms and related fees paid, signed, sealed and delivered. How many more forms and fees are there?" I complained in return.

"This is the last form, but the most important. You must wire me that money so that I can deliver it to the security company. They will send to you the form. You must sign it, then send it back to me. That is the only way I can sign the papers for you. This is most important, Mr. Wizard. Do not fail us now. We are so close to delivering the money into your account.

"You must also fax to me your bank account details, so that I can transfer the money into your account. You must also wire me the thirty-five hundred dollars to open up the Special Domiciliary Account at the bank in Cotonou, if you want me to do that for you, as well," David instructed with authority.

I detected a distinct raise in David's voice when he asked, "Why are you making this transaction so difficult? Perhaps we chose wrong in requesting your assistance. We are willing to pay you a lot of money for your help. Do not fail us now."

Wow, what a guilt trip. It didn't stop there, either.

Turning the volume up one more notch, David spoke. "As you know, Mohammed is in prison, where conditions are not good. His health is failing and his mother is worried he will die in prison. He has killed no one, but still he is held in prison. How can you turn your back on him in his time of need?"

"David, I'm not turning my back on him. There are some things you are not taking into consideration. Like the fifteen hundred dollars here, and seven hundred and twenty there, with another thirty-five hundred to boot. It's all adding up to a huge sum of money. Money out of *my* pocket. Out of my *wife's* pocket. Out of my *business* pocket. That's a lot to ask of me."

"Okay, Mr. Wizard, I am sorry I raised my voice. It is just that I am worried about Mohammed, and what they are doing to him in that prison. Send me the documents you are drafting and I will see what I can do with them."

I couldn't guess what my phone bill was going to be from all of this international calling, but I did know I hate being yelled at for free, never mind paying for it. Especially by a scam artist! Nonetheless, I drafted the power of attorney, had it notarized, and waited until later in the day, when I knew David's office would have the fax machine answering the phone.

I stopped by the pub to chat with Dennis, and give him an update on my investigation into the Nigerian story.

"Now they want a cool fifteen hundred for one thing and another thirty-five hundred for something else. Got an extra few thousand you can loan me?" I asked in jest.

"Not this month," Dennis replied with a smile. "What are you going to do?"

"Bullshit the bullshitters."

* * *

At home, I had started working on my new outbuilding. I had many windows, so a greenhouse sounded logical, except I lack a green thumb. I decided to construct an all-purpose outbuilding. This project demanded much of my time. I was racing the weather. Winter was right around the corner. It was almost a week before I returned to the scam artists. Rolled up in front of the fax machine was the CO2 form.

CLEARANCE / ASSESSMENT FORM
CO2 - AX - 107 - BG.

IN RATIFICATION WITH THE VERIFICATION EXERCISE BY THE P. I. M. BANK IN CONJUNCTION WITH THE DIPLOMATIC CHANNEL ESTABLISHED UNDER THE GUIDE LINE AND REGULATION OF DECREE (54) SECTION 2 OF 1998.

AS A PRE - REQUISITE IN LINE WITH YOUR CLAIMS AND VALUE. YOU ARE REQUESTED TO GO FOR THE CLAIMS OF YOUR MONEY US$25M TRANSFERRED CASH TO TRANSWORLD SECURITIES COMPANY BENIN (COTONOU). DO UP DATE THE FOLLOWING FILL THE SPACE STAMP AND SIGN AND FAX SAME BACK THROUGH YOUR REPRESENTATIVE.

A. THE BENEFICIARY'S

NAME: BRIAN Wizard

ADDRESS: POB 43 Waltina Or. USA

TEL & FAX NO: 541 886 4025

BENEFICIARY STAMP & SIGN

OFFICE USE ONLY

CHAIRMANS RECOMMENDATION / APPROVAL RELEASE CASH TO BRIAN WIZARD.

TYPE OF REMITTANCE: WIRE [ ] CASH [✓] CHEQUE [ ]

TAXES [PAID ✓] NON PAID [ ]

FILE NO. [744] ITEM APPROVAL NO. [3155]

TOTAL AMOUNT US $ 25 M.

On the e-mail was a note from Mo:

mohameduz abacha,10/20/99 4:28 PM -0700,Re:GET IT DONE..

```
X-From_: mohameduz@mailcity.com  Wed Oct 20 16:29:45 1999
To: bwizard@eoni.com
Date: Wed, 20 Oct 1999 23:28:31  0000
From: "mohameduz abacha" <mohameduz@mailcity.com>
Mime-Version: 1.0
X-Sent-Mail: off
Subject: Re:GET IT DONE..
X-Sender-Ip: 208.243.226.224
Organization: MailCity  (http://www.mailcity.lycos.com:80)

  ATTN; WIZARD.

WHERE WELL HAVE YOU GONE WITH DAVID TO CONCLUDE THIS TRASACTION.

I WILL THIS TRANSACTION TO BE OVER THIS WEEK.

HE  DAVID TOLD ME ABOUT MONEY TO GET BACK TO BENIN WHICH HE SAID WILL COST HIM $4,000
TRY ALL YOU CAN TO ARANGE THIS FUND FOR HIM TO CONCLUDE THIS TRANSACTION THIS WEEK.

I ALSO TOLD HIM TO ADD MORE MONEY TO YOUR PERCENTAGE SINCE YOU ARE MAKING MUCH CALL AS

DO COST YOU ALOT OF MONEY SO DAVID TOLD ME.

I AM SURE WITH YOU THE TRANSACTION WILL BE CONCLUDED THIS WEEK.

THANKS.
```

This e-mail was Mo's worst yet in terms of his English syntax. The good news was: He gave me a five percent raise. The bad news was: A large percentage of nothing is still nothing. More bad news was that I wasn't sending David any money. That would be bad news for him. I called to let him know.

"David, Brian Wizard. Is this a convenient time for you to talk?"

"Mr. Wizard, it is always convenient for me to talk to you."

"I received the CO_2 form," I confirmed. "I'll sign it, then fax it to your office tonight. Good?"

"Yes, but you might have to fax it to me again in Cotonou. I am afraid to take such documents across the border," David told me. "What I need you to do for me now is to send me as much money as you can, so that I can travel to Cotonou and reside in a good hotel. I will need enough money for two rooms. Prince Madu will be with me once I arrive. He must have his own room."

"He can buy his own room," I countered. "He's the prince." Prince of what? I didn't have a clue.

"No. He has no money. He is with me on this business. He is family, an in-law," David disclosed.

Whoops, David. Mistake. The prince was Mo's in-law, not yours. I was sure that Mo had claimed the prince as his in-law in one of his e-mails. Things were getting rather complicated. That was good. A rule of combat: Make a simple matter out of the complicated by looking at the bigger picture.

I looked at the bigger picture and saw a growing network. A family was being born. A family of fools and outlaws that lived in the weird world of the scam.

My internal dialog made me fall silent. David broke the silence, saying, "You must send me some money. Can you do that?"

"David. Did I tell you my wife left me? She's pissed at me, you, and Mo. She found out I sent you money. She thinks you and Mo are scam artists. Ever hear of the 419 Scam that originates in Nigeria?"

"Yes, I have," David admitted. "We are not the scam. I promise. When you receive this first batch of twenty-five million dollars you will see that, and you will have many women."

I laughed. "That's just great, David. Like I said before, though, you must make things happen on the end of the . . ." and I almost said "scam" but caught myself just in time . . . "deal."

"Try, Mr. Wizard. Try for Mohammed and his family. He is dying in that prison. When we collect this money we will be able to help him get out of jail. You will get your wife back, too."

"We'll see what happens, David. I'll fax you the signed CO2." We left it at that.

This investigation was starting to wear on my mind. How dangerous was this? When would the CIA, FBI, British Intelligence, Interpol and the Nigerian Secret Hit Squad step in? What exactly were the lies? Did the newspaper articles support the truth? David must have been monitoring the news daily so that he could use it to create or support his lies. The Nigerian News Network verified the details David told me about Mohammed Abacha: Mohammed's ill health, his continued detention, his alleged crimes, his mother's worry, his cohorts' similar ordeal. I even found this article that shed a not-so-nice light upon our Mohammed:

COVER STORIES

Mohammed - A chip
off the old block

The Tyrant's Son

Mohammed Abacha, as greedy and unfeeling like his father, faces the heat as President Obasanjo searches for the country's stolen billions

By OSA DIRECTOR

For those who are privy to the mindset of the President Olusegun Obasanjo administration, the invitation, two weeks ago, of Maryam and Mohammed Abacha to Aso Rock did not come as a surprise. Mother and son have featured prominently as the arrow-heads in the looting of the nation's treasury that was perpetrated during the inglorious reign of the late dictator, General Sani Abacha. The retired Lieutenant-General Mohammed Aliyu Gusau-led panel on the recovery of looted monies and properties, during its recent trip abroad, stumbled on fresh evidence implicating the former first family. More so, the attempt by the Gusau team to open negotiations with the banks and financial institutions where the monies are stashed met with a brickwall deliberately erected by Mohammed Abacha, who was last week arrested by security agents in Kano. The arrest comes in the wake of the trial of Major Hamza Al-Mustapha and Sergeant Rogers Mshelia, General Abacha's CSO

and security operative respectively. They are charged for the murders of Kudirat Abiola, Alfred Rewane, the torture of political prisoners during the indescribably evil reign of Mohammed's father, General Abacha. Mohammed, sources, and surviving victims say, participated very actively in Al-Mustapha's and Rogers' sadistic acts.

A reliable source, who spoke to TELL, indicated that fresh pieces of evidence are linking Mohammed with the illegal transfer of the sum of $2.2 billion into different accounts abroad. And a large portion of this amount was siphoned through the amorphous but octopodal Family Economic Advancement Programme. FEAP, which was under the total control and supervision of the erstwhile 'First Lady,' Maryam. The FEAP, established by Decree 11 of 1997, was given an initial take-off grant of N1.07 billion. But within a year of its operations, the junta had budgeted N5.18 billion for it to disburse as loans for small-scale enterprises. Most of the monies were diverted into private accounts through bogus expenditures. Also, a lot of FEAP allocation was being diverted from outside the federal purse were channelled into the foreign bank accounts of Maryam and Mohammed through the bogus plan of importation of vaccines and drugs for the poor. The stolen $2.2 billion was also said to have emanated from some contracts awarded to Mohammed which were not executed. Such contracts include the $32 million contract for the supply of vaccines for the Expanded Programme on Immunisation, EPI and the national debt buy-back scam.

Hence, when Maryam and Mohammed were summoned to Aso Rock, they met with Vice-President Abubakar Atiku, who advised them to fully co-operate with the government in its recovery efforts. Atiku expressed displeasure at the present "unsatisfactory conduct and uncooperative attitude of the Abachas in returning the country's looted wealth. The extravagance and obscene opulence, which smacks of unremorsefulness, displayed by the Abachas during the recent wedding of two of their daughters had also raised eyebrows in high quarters. Such unremorseful attitude was the issue, sources say, Maryam was also warned about. Though the discussion with Atiku were frank and courteous. Maryam, reportedly wept for her characteristic unperturbed manner, told confidants that she was embarrassed by the encounter with Atiku. She had expected to meet with President Obasanjo. However, Mohammed, who was delayed further for another day in Abuja, was politely told of the consequences of stonewalling to frustrate the recovery plan. TELL learnt that rougher measures await them.

Maryam – the remorseful matriarch of the Abacha family

Abacha – 'Commander-in-thief'

Early Friday morning I had to stop work on my new outbuilding because I had run out of nails. I went to town on this errand, but soon realized that this was just an excuse to check my e-mails and faxes.

As I entered my office I quickly scanned the table top in front of the fax machine. Nothing. In my e-mail I found:

mohameduz abacha,10/22/99 11:18 PM -0700,Re: TRIP TO BENIN..

```
X-From_: mohameduz@mailcity.com  Fri Oct 22 23:19:03 1999
To: bwizard@eoni.com
Date: Sat, 23 Oct 1999 06:18:15  0000
From: "mohameduz abacha" <mohameduz@mailcity.com>
Mime-Version: 1.0
X-Sent-Mail: off
X-Expiredinmiddle: true
Subject: Re: TRIP TO BENIN..
X-Sender-Ip: 208.243.226.224
Organization: MailCity  (http://www.mailcity.lycos.com:80)

ATTN; BRIAN WIZARD.

DAVID WILL BE GOING TO BENIN ON MONDAY WITH OUT MUCH MONEY TO FINALISE WHAT HE IS GOING THERE FOR. HE
TOLD ME YOU PROMISED TO SEND SOME MONEY TO HIM BUT ALL FIALED  I DON'T KNOW WHY ALL THIS.

DO CALL DAVID ON MONEY AT BENIN AT THE SAME HOTEL VICK KINFEL  ON TELL NO; 229- 31 -38-14. LODGED IN
WITH MY IN LAW'S NAME. PRINCE UZOMA MADU.

CALL HIM IF YOUARE NOT AT HOME TO TALK WITH HIM.

HE WILL COLLECT ALL REQUIRED DOCUMENTS FROM YOU WHILE IN BENIN.

YOU NEEN TO CALL HIM. AS YOUR CALL WILL ENABLE
THE TRANSFER TO BE EFFECTED IN YOUR NAME. CALL DAVID NOW.

.M.ABACHA.
```

I went home with nails in hand, and a mission: Wait for Monday.

*   *   *

It was a long weekend waiting for Monday. In a breach of my standard rule, do not bring office work home, I couldn't help myself from thinking about the developing plot concerning stolen Nigerian wealth. Perhaps I was part of the largest international conspiracy to launder stolen wealth, ever.

Was it illegal to volunteer to become a victim of an attempted scam?

What if I did receive big money? That would be an overwhelming responsibility. What would I do?

On Monday morning I found a fax from Trans-World Security's Koffie Biyah rolled up on the table. The document had an odd array of ink spots over it. By the look of the splatter pattern I guessed that it was blood from some poor bastard after he took a head shot from a medium caliber pistol.

TRANS - WORLD SECURITY COMPANY

COTONOU - REPUBLIQUE DU BENIN
RUE DE CARREFOUR
01 BP 2634 RECETTE DE JERICHO
TEL/FAX : 229 - 33 - 70 - 66

Cotonou, 2nd OCTOBER 1999

ATTN: MR BRIAN WILLARD
BRIAN WIZARD
U.S.A.

Dear Mr. BRIAN WILLARD,

This is to acknowledge the receipt of your fax messages dated 30/00/00. The contents therein is quite clear and understood. Your present health condition had made our company Policy of Payment on personal presentation for identification purposes and signing of all original documents by the Bonafide Beneficiary in the presence of the Bank Officials and TWSC Officials. Due to your present health condition, this our payment policy is now reversed and this purely based on humanitarian consideration.

After a closed-door meeting of Management about your present 100% total permanent disability condition and due to medical facilities in Benin is limited to cases of your condition on any emergency. Your request for **Mr. David Olatunde** your Attorney in Nigeria to act as your Sole Representative had been granted on the following conditions :

1°) That you are now required to send via DHL Courrier Services the original copy of the Special Power of Attorney for **Mr. David OLATUNDE** to act on your behalf with four - passport size photographs (signed behind by you) and 2 copies of your confirmed Banking particulars in U.S.A. on your Company letter-headed paper where the funds would be T.T. from the Bank Account to be opened on your behalf by **David Olatunde** your Attorney

2°) That the duties of your Attorney would be limited only on these areas.

a) Opening of the Special Dollar Domiciliary Account on your behalf.

b) Deposit and Transfer of the funds in full as per your Standing Order No DEDUCTIONS whatsoever.

c) Signing of all Original Bank Transfer Documents, Transworld Security Documents, Ministry of Finance Documents i.e. T.T.C.C., Remittance– Order Form, Diplomatic Channel Center Receipt of Clearance etc... on your behalf.

3°) For an effective conclusion of your Payment in the presence of your Attorney in Cotonou, you are now required to send via Western Union Money Transfer or we forward to you our Company Bank Account In U.S.A., the following funds before the arrival of your Attorney in Cotonou, while you advice your Attorney on this new arrangements.

a) US $ 3,500 for the opening of the Special Dollar Domicillary Account on your behalf.

b) US $ 12,700 for the Telegraphic Transfer Clearance Certificate (T.T.C.C.) from the Ministry of Finance on your behalf.

c) US $ 2,500 for Security Bullion Van Transportation Charges which will convey the money to the Bank for counting and deposit on your behalf.

d) US $ 2,850 for Swearing of Affidavit and Stamp Duty from the Ministry of Justice to legalize the funds transfer and in compliance with the Monetary laws of the Republic of Benin on your behalf.

Meanwhile you should also sign the beneficiary column of the Certificate of Ownership faxed to you, and fax same to this office as well as your 1st and 2nd pages of your International Passport for record purposes.

Finally, if you agree with the new decision as unanimously reached and agreed by the Management of Transworld Security Company to assist you without your travelling to Cotonou, you should confirm your acceptance of this decision by a return Fax message to enable us forward you the address where you would send the DHL parcel and the details of the Western Union Money Transfer or Our Company Bank details in U.S.A. Treat this as very urgent.

Thanks for your kind understanding and co-operation and be assured of the best of our services for the Final Release of your funds now in our Security Vault via T.T. on receipt of the above requirements.

My Personal Best Regards.

MR. KOFFI M. BIYAH
(Director : Delivery & Operations)

B. ANJORIN
2/10/99
(Accountant)

46

Good news! My presence was no longer necessary in Benin. "Excused on *humanitarian consideration*," I proudly read out loud. They had bought it.

The bad news was an itemized demand for more money that totaled up to $21,550 U.S. Whew! No more nickel and dime requests. This had to be the last push for my money.

On the e-mail was this note from Mo:

mohameduz abacha,10/27/99 11:32 AM +0100,Re: TRIP TO BENIN   1

```
X-From_: mohameduz@mailcity.com  Wed Oct 27 03:33:57 1999
To: bwizard@eoni.com
Date: Wed, 27 Oct 1999 10:32:52  0000
From: "mohameduz abacha" <mohameduz@mailcity.com>
Mime-Version: 1.0
X-Sent-Mail: on
Subject: Re: TRIP TO BENIN
X-Sender-Ip: 208.243.226.224
Organization: MailCity  (http://www.mailcity.lycos.com:80)

ATTN;BRIAN

DAVID SENT HIS LAWYER TO ME TELLING ME THAT THE FAX YOU SENT WAS RECIVED BUT THE SIGNATURE IS NOT THE
SAME AS YOU SIGN BEFORE THAT YOU SHOULD TRY AND CALL HIM ON THIS NUMBER 229-31-38-14
PLEASE TRY AND COPERATE FOR THE TRANSACTION IS ALMOST OVER.

THANKS


M.ABACHA
```

I called David at the hotel in Cotonou. "David, Brian Wizard."

"Oh, Mr. Wizard," David moaned. "Why are you doing this to us? Who signed the CO2 Form? It was not your signature."

"Yes it was!" I adamantly stood my ground. "What's your problem? Are you going to close this deal, or not?"

"I don't know how," the defeatist said. "Where am I going to get the money for fees? I have sold all of my cars, even my Landrover. I cannot go to my office in the city anymore. Men I borrowed money from are looking for me there."

"You've got to do something, my friend. I told you that everything on your end of the stick has to be handled by you. Do you realize the work you are expecting me to do once the money is in my possession?" I was thinking on my feet, or buttocks, so to speak. I wondered if David was aware of the magnitude of the financial responsibility he was trying to impose me. I would become a slave to this money. I would have to control it daily with investments, taxes, and accounting.

"Look, David, you are the hero in this transaction. You can't be the hero if you are always asking me to do your work for you. You won't be here when I'm busting my butt monitoring all this money. I've given you my account numbers, my time, and a lot of cash already. My phone bill alone is fifteen hundred dollars. This whole idea is yours. You and Mo have to work that end. I'm way over here. Now pull yourself together and make things work. You have my power of attorney. You can make this happen. You can do it, buddy. You and only you. You're the man!"

Before I could let David discount my inspirational rally, I said, "Hey, there's someone at my door. This is important. I have to go. You must make all things happen."

*   *   *

I waited for David to call, or Mo to send an e-mail telling me David had concluded the transaction. It sure would be grand to have twenty-five million to play with. It would be play, not work. It would be other people's money! I couldn't lose. To my disappointment, not a word came from any Nigerian for days. I had to write Mo:

mohameduz abacha,5/30/00 6:33 AM -0700,Re: TRIP TO BENIN.   1

```
      To: "mohameduz abacha" <mohameduz@mailcity.com>
    From: Brian Wizard <bwizard@pop3.eoni.com>
 Subject: Re: TRIP TO BENIN.
      Cc:
     Bcc:
X-Attachments:
```

Mo,
        So, did David come through like the hero he is, or did he whimp out in the end? I called him in Benin. I faxed him the papers. He got pissy about me not sending any more money. It might have been easier convincing a rock to bleed. My sales trip was not financially fruitful, and I sort of need some reassurance that what you guys have going is not a 419 scam. I also feel that you should be handling things on your end. Later, when the financial ball is passed to me, I will work my butt to the bone making all things flow smoothly.
        Needless to say, here I sit waiting to hear about David's success and how the ball will be kicked my way without further delay.
        So, how's life in the big house? I'm amazed that you have e-mail access. You must be pampered, all things considered.
        Keep in touch. Whatever happens. I don't think our buisness is over, even if you fail to follow through on your operations. I shall be watching my account for a deposit.
                Brian Wizard

I could hardly wait to hear what he had to say about being called a 419 scamster. Tipping my hand as to my ability to write stories might make Mo back off. Perhaps he would fear exposure if I wrote about him. Probably not, since this Mohammed Abacha was a fictitious character.

* * *

The next day I received this note from Mo:

mohameduz abacha,10/31/99 3:51 AM +0100,Re: TRIP TO BENIN.   **1**

```
X-From_: mohameduz@mailcity.com  Sat Oct 30 20:52:50 1999
To: bwizard@eoni.com
Date: Sun, 31 Oct 1999 02:51:25  0000
From: "mohameduz abacha" <mohameduz@mailcity.com>
Mime-Version: 1.0
X-Sent-Mail: off
Subject: Re: TRIP TO BENIN.
X-Sender-Ip: 208.243.226.224
Organization: MailCity  (http://www.mailcity.lycos.com:80)

ATTN BRAIN

I HAVE KNOWN AND HEARD ALL THE 419 PERSON I AM I  WILL NEVER BLAME YOU IT ALL CAME BACUASE OF MY LATE
FATHER.

PLEASE IF YOU DON'T WANT TO CONTINUE BETTER SEND TO DAVID A POWER OF ATTORNEY  STATING THAT YOU DON'T WANT
TO CONTINUE WITH THIS TRASACTION ANY MORE.THAT I SHOULD LOOK FOR SOME ONE.


I WILL WANT  YOU TELL ME HOW MUCH YOU HAVE SPENT BOTH ON  YOUR CALLS, FAXES AND CASH I PROMISE TO PAY YOU
BACK AS SOON AS THE  MONEY IS INTO SOME ONES ACCOUNT.

BUT PLEASE DON'T CALL ME OR DAVID A 419 MAN.

THANK YOU

M.ABACHA.
```

It was good to hear him say that neither he, nor David was a 419 man. Backing out of this investigation did not interest me. I was hooked.

Reimbursement for expenses sounded good, although I had my doubts a penny would ever materialize.

I wasn't going to send the twenty-some grand, that was for sure. I didn't mind researching the scam, or even playing along a little bit just to keep the story going, but I was not going to be scammed big time. What more could I do? I could only wait for David to come through.

I decided to send this note to Mo:

49

Mo,

I am afraid we are at an impasse, my friend. I would like to do more for you than I already have, but I can't come up with the $21,550. Sorry. We both must pray that David will come through for us. I sit here, ready to jump into action as soon as the money arrives. I have explained to David that he is the hero on that end of the stick. Success rests in his hands, not mine, not yours. I don't know what else to tell you until I hear the sound of the cash register at my bank sing, "Ka-ching!"

SECOND CONTACT

Martin entered my office on the following Saturday afternoon. He was curious about the African story. "What's up with the Africans?"

"Mo is still in jail, and it looks as if he'll be there for a while." I passed Martin a news article on Mo's latest predicament.

Vanguard: 2nd Lead Story

Return to Vanguard front page

By Ise-Oluwa Ige

LAGOS State Justice Ministry yesterday filed a fresh criminal proceeding at an Ikeja High Court against the Chief Security Officer to the late General Sani Abacha, Major Hamza Al-Mustapha, Abacha's son, Mohammed and three others.

Also yesterday at the Ikeja High Court, Mohammed's lawyer filed an application for his release on bail.

Mohammed and the other four are currently standing trial at an Ikeja Chief Magistrate Court for the July 4, 1996 murder of Alhaja Kudirat Abiola.

That trial is expected to continue today.

Details of the fresh proceeding filed yesterday were, however, not immediately available.

Standing trial with Mohammed are Al-Mustapha, Aminu Mohammed, a Chief Superintendent of Police, Mohammed Rabo and Chief Protocol Officer to late Alhaja Abiola, Alhaji Lateef Shofolahan.

No plea was taken when they appeared before the court on October 14, this year.

The fresh proceeding against the accused persons was filed by the Lagos State Director of Public Prosecution, Mrs. Ngozi Mofunnaya.

A source close to the Justice Ministry told *Vanguard* that the action was murder related and would be heard before December 3, this year.

The source said the action was accompanied by a letter addressed to Chief Magistrate A. B. Oke-Lawal who is billed to hear the five-count charge of murder preferred against the accused persons this morning, notifying him of the decision of the state's Justice Minister to formally take over the prosecution of all the accused persons.

On what exactly would become of the murder charge against Major Mustapha and others at the Chief Magistrate Court with the institution of fresh murder charges the source said:

"The matter will still come up at the Chief Magistrate Court tomorrow morning (today). It will only be mentioned and the Chief Magistrate who has now been duly notified vide a letter from the office of the state's Director of Public Prosecution of its intention to prosecute the matter will now fix a short adjourned date. For sure, if it cannot be earlier than December 3 or thereabout.

"But," the source added, "before the adjourned date, a date would have been fixed by an Ikeja High Court for the commencement of hearing in the matter when all the suspects would now be properly arraigned before a high court of jurisdiction with their pleas taken to allow

Page: 1

trial commence in the matter."

The source went further to explain "so, on the fixed adjourned date by the Ikeja Chief Magistrate Court in December, the prosecution would just appear to inform the court of its intention to withdraw the matter on the grounds that a court of proper jurisdiction has taken up the matter and it would be accordingly struck out on the consent of both parties."

"Murder!" Martin exclaimed, as he read the charges against Mo. "That doesn't sound very promising. Without this guy, you won't be able to get the money, will you?"

I looked hard at Martin. I knew he realized this money was non-existent. But that is exactly how a scam succeeds. You want to believe in it. "There is no money," I reminded him.

"Damn!" Martin complained. "Wish this weren't a scam. I can dream, can't I?"

"The dream of financial freedom is the backbone of scams," I explained. "Everything would change, though. No more scuffling."

"You'd set me up with my own knife factory, wouldn't you?" Martin asked for reconfirmation of an earlier suggestion I had made.

"We'd have a huge shop, with all the latest in tools and toys," I promised him. "The real question would be, where? There's no reason why you have to continue to live in the fog. Or in the cold north. Or even live in America. I'm thinking Belize. Warm. Tropical. English-speaking Belize."

"That sounds good to me," Martin concurred. On a low note, he added, "So, it's over?"

"The dream will never be over," I assured him, hoping to lift his spirits. "There's always the lottery."

Martin smiled. "I've got a ticket for the next draw."

I told Martin, "I guess Mo and David aren't talking to me anymore since I'm not putting any more money into their pockets. If they paid me the expense money they promised, I'd give it all back to them. Let them scam themselves. Perhaps a quick note to Mo reminding him about the expense money will wake him up."

Martin watched me create this note:

Mo,

I read in the paper that you are still in prison. No chance of escape, eh?

What about sending me that money to cover my expenses, like you said you would? $10,000 would be about right.

Yours truly,
Brian Wizard

PS: I am still waiting for the transfer of the money into my account. What is David doing about that? Is he using the power of attorney I gave him to overcome the obstacles?

*   *   *

The following Monday I received a letter sent from the Republique De Guinee. This letter was written by a man named Abu Abubarka:

Federal Government of Nigeria
Contract Review Committee
Federal Secretariat Lagos - Abuja

From the desk of:	**Alhaji Abu *Abubakar***	***Tel/Fax:***	234-1-7742491
	Head, Contract Review Committee	*Fax:*	234-1-2881108
		Fax:	234-90-409498

REQUEST FOR URGENT BUSINESS RELATIONSHIP
RE: TRANSFER OF US$25,320,000.00 ONLY (AMERICAN DOLLARS) INTO YOUR ACCOUNT

BY WAY OF SELF-IDENTIFICATION, I AM THE CHAIRMAN OF THE ADHOC COMMITTEE SET-UP BY THE PRESENT CIVILIAN GOVERNMENT OF THE FEDERAL REPUBLIC OF NIGERIA TO REVIEW, APPRAISE, AND FINALIZE DETAILS OF VARIOUS MULTI-MILLION DOLLARS CONTRACTS PAYMENT AWARDED BY THE PAST MILITARY REGIMES BETWEEN 1984-1999.

IN THE COURSE OF CARRYING OUT OUR ASSIGNMENT, WE HAVE DISCOVERED THAT THERE ARE FUNDS CURRENTLY FLOATING IN THE CENTRAL BANK OF NIGERIA (CBN) / NIGERIAN NATIONAL PETROLEUM CORPORATION (NNPC) FOREIGN PAYMENT ACCOUNT. AS RESULT OF THIS PLEASANT DISCOVERING, AND CONSIDERING THE FACT THAT ESTABLISHING A BUSINESS RELATIONSHIP WITH YOU AND YOUR COMPANY AS FACILITATORS. IN LINE WITH THIS, WE STRONGLY SOLICIT YOUR PARTNERSHIP TO ENABLE US TRANSFER INTO YOUR ACCOUNT THE SAID FUNDS. YOU ARE RECOMMENDED TO US IN CONFIDENCE AND WITH THE ASSURANCE OF POSSESSING REQUIRED ABILITY TO CONDUCT BUSINESS TRANSACTIONS WITH UTMOST CONFIDENTIALITY.

ORIGIN OF FUNDS: THE FUNDS WHICH ARE CURRENTLY FLOATING IN THE NNPC FOREIGN PAYMENT ACCOUNT WITH THE CBN, ARE AS A RESULT OF GROSSLY OVER- INVOICED CONTRACTS WHICH WERE EXECUTED FOR THE NNPC DURING THE MILITARY ERA IN QUESTION CURRENTLY UNDER VERIFICATION. THE ORIGINAL COMPANIES WHICH EXECUTED THAT CONTRACTS HAVE BEEN FULLY PAID LEAVING THE SUM OF **US$25,320,000.00 (TWENTY FIVE MILLION, THREE HUNDRED AND TWENTY THOUSAND DOLLARS)** IN THE FLOATING ACCOUNT WHICH WE INTEND TO TRANSFER INTO YOUR ACCOUNT WITH MAXIMUM CO-OPERATION. FOLLOWING THE EXPEDIENCY AND THE NEED FOR CAUTION IN SOURCING FOR A TRUST WORTHY CONFIDANT AS A FOREIGN PARTNER INTO WHOSE ACCOUNT WE CAN TRANSFER THE SUM OF **US$25,320,000.00** I WAS MANDATED TO CONTACT YOU HENCE I AM WRITING THIS LETTER FOR PURPOSES OF CLARITY, THE PROJECTED AGREED SHARING FORMULA FOR ALL PARTNERS INVOLVED IN THIS FUNDS TRANSFER TRANSACTION IS AS FOLLOWS:-

1. 65% FOR US (THE COMMITTEE MEMBERS)
2. 25% FOR ACCOUNT OWNER (THAT IS YOU)
3. 10% FOR THE SETTLING OF PREPAYMENT EXPENSES AS IN TAXATION AND ALL LOCAL AND FOREIGN EXPENSES WHICH MAY BE INCURRED IN THE COURSE OF EXECUTING THIS TRANSACTION.

AS A HEADSTART, WE INTEND TO ARRANGE THE IMPORTATION OF GOODS WITH OUR SHARE OF THE TRANSFERRED FUNDS IN DOING THIS, WE SHALL DEPEND ON YOUR ASSISTANCE AS WELL AS ADVICE. WE SHALL COMMENCE THE PROCESSING OF THE FUNDS TRANSFER IMMEDIATELY WE RECEIVE THE FOLLOWING REQUISITE INFORMATION USING OUR TEL/FAX LINES ABOVE:

1. YOUR COMPANY'S NAME, FULL ADDRESS, TELEPHONE AND FAX NUMBERS
2. YOUR BANKER'S NAME, ADDRESS, TELEPHONE AND FAX NUMBERS
3. TH ACCOUNT NUMBER AND NAME OF WOULD BE BENEFICIARY.

ABOVE REQUESTED INFORMATION WOULD ENABLE US PUT TOGETHER LETTERS OF JOB DESCRIPTION, EXECUTION AND CLAIMS TO THE RESPECTIVE MINISTRIES TO ENSURE AND FACILITATE THE ISSUANCE OF MANDATORY FUND RELEASE RECOMMENDATIONS AND APPROVALS. THIS WILL AUTOMATICALLY BESTOW ON YOUR COMPANY THE STATUS OF THE BONAFIDE BENEFICIARY OF THE CONTRACT ENTITLEMENT BEFORE THE FINAL REMITTANCE INTO YOUR NOMINATED ACCOUNT BY THE CENTRAL BANK OF NIGERIA.

AS A MATTER OF NECESSITY, I WISH TO ASSURE YOU OF THE FLAWLESSNESS OF THIS ARRANGEMENT DUE TO OUR PERFECTION OF SAME THERE IS NOTHING TO WORRY ABOUT IN TERMS OF ITS WORKABILITY. INFACT, THE LAW UNDER WHICH OUR COMMITTEE IS SET-UP EMPOWERS US TO DISBURSE ALL FUNDS FOUND FLOATING IN ANY OF THE FOREIGN PAYMENT ACCOUNT KEPT WITH THE CBN. PLEASE, WE LOOK FORWARD TO DOING BUSINESS WITH YOU, AND DO ALSO SOLICIT YOUR ABSOLUTE CONFIDENTIALITY DURING THIS TRANSACTION. KINDLY ACKNOWLEDGE RECEIPT OF THIS LETTER USING THE TEL/FAX LINES AS GIVEN ABOVE FOR MORE DETAILS REGARDING THIS TRANSACTION.

PLEASE TREAT WITH UTMOST CONFIDENTIALITY AND URGENCY.

YOURS FAITHFULLY,

ABU ABUBAKAR

My interest skyrocketed when I read that another allocation of twenty-five million, and change, was slated for transfer into my account. "These Nigerians have money coming out of their socks!" I remarked. I had to share this news with someone. I went to the pub.

When Dennis saw me walk in, his first words were, "Got any of that African money yet?"

"Not yet," I told him. "But I did receive another offer for more free money. A completely different player." I showed Dennis the latest communiqué from Nigeria, by way of Guinee.

"Are you going to send this guy any money?" Dennis asked.

"No. I did enough sending of money to David. It bought me some unique wallpaper, but that was about it. I do intend on following up on this, though. Experienced as I am, my research should be more cost effective."

"Good to hear that." Dennis's voice was upbeat. "Here." Dennis passed me my bar tab for the past two months.

"Can't you wait until I get the Nigerian money?" I asked, but Dennis's expression canceled that hope.

Returned to my office, I drafted this letter to Abu:

Mr. Abubakar,

Congratulations for enlisting my talent in your quest for an entrepreneurial partner. You have selected well.

Now, above and below are the details you requested in order to transfer the 25 millio US dollars into my control.

Your timing is perfect. I am immediately leaving to visit Hong Kong for business details in forming a film production company for the China Television Broadcast Network will be gone for two to six weeks, depending on how things go. I should hope to return to fi the completion of the money transfer into my account, and suggestions on what you want to do for you in the investment end of your proposal.

I'm sure you have the talent and arrangement to pay all fees and make all the details stamped, signed, notarized, etc. without my assistance. Of course, you have my permission extract from the funds all relative fees, (the ten percent your letter mentions).

I will have my secretary monitor the bank account for the deposit. Perhaps there is something from Asia you would like for me to look into. Please, let me know through my secretary if there is anything you need in that regards.

I do hope to find us working partners in the near future. As I said, your timing is perfect. After this latest business deal in Asia, I haven't anything exciting written in concrete for the winter's projects. Winter is a good time for me to focus on investments. Let the magic begin. SEND THE MONEY!

> Yours truly,
> Brian Wizard

Bank Account Details:

Klamath First Federal
106 S.W. First St.
Enterprise, Or. 97828
Phone: USA 541 426 3124
Fax: 541 426 4747
Routing Number, including account number: 323 270 300   48 70043751
Name of Beneficiary: Brian Wizard

I could only wait and see what response that fax to Abu would bring. I threw in the China material to buy some time, and to create an image of a very busy international businessman. I did some quick math: 25 mill, plus 25,320,000, makes a cool $50,320,000. That would make some dreams come true. Since my raise with David went from twenty percent to twenty-five, and here was another twenty-five percent, I would soon have twelve million and some dollars of my own. My mother always told me, "You are such a dreamer."

*   *   *

Tuesday didn't bring a response from Abu, but Wednesday did. I found a phone message waiting for me. Unfortunately, I couldn't understand it due to the low volume of the recording. The fax was clear, though. It read:

Federal Government of Nigeria
Contract Review Committee
Federal Secretariat, Lagos - Abuja.

MEMO

From the desk of: **Alhaji Abu Abubarka**	*Tel/Fax No:234-1-2881108*
Head, Contract Review Committee	*Fax: 234-90-409498*

To: Brian Wizard	*Date:* 11/11/99

CONFIDENTIAL FAX MESSAGE

I must apologise for responding late to your fax correspondence of 8th November, 1999. I was out of my workstation on an official assignment.

I wish to also thank you for your response to my business proposal. I had communicated with you basically on behalf of the Contract Review Committee (CRC) which I head. The functional details of the proposal as had been superficially presented and the modalities for its speedy realisation will be spelt out shortly.

The Contract Review Committee (CRC) is a body set up by the Federal Government of Nigeria, and primarily charged with the responsibilities of scrutinizing awarded contracts with a view to determininig contractual claims, and making payment recommendation(s) to the National Economic Intelligence Commission (NEIC) for final settlement.

On the basis of this mandate which we control, we are favourably disposed to giving absolute approval for the payment of the outstanding contract sum of $25,320,000.00 in favour of your company. To justify this transaction as it is, appropiate documentation reflecting an original award of the contract to your company as well as other processes of completion of the contract would be made available promptly and adequately. This readily gives the transaction the due legal backing it desires.

The due process of the National Economic Intelligence Commission (NEIC) updating you on the status of payment will be effective from the date we submit our recommendation notice. The NEIC is the body responsible for the final release of approved contract sum for payment. As soon as payment is effected to your nominated Bank Account, I shall arrange tocome over to U.S.A. to meet with you for the disbursement, and commence at once our importation concern as indicated in our letter of business proposal.

I have taken note of your travelling plan and beg that you remain in contact touch with you secretary so that you can be abreadst with developments. You should try your best possible while in China to call me on my telefax number; 234-1-2881108 so that will can rub minds together on developments .

I am assuring you that at the successful completion of this laudable transaction, our lives will never be the same and a long lasting relationship will be established between us and our immediate family members.I see us spending the winter period doing good business.

During your stay in China, I will advice that you take time out and enquiry about the cost of agicultural farming implements like, tractors, planters, havesters, et.c, so that we can compare with the ones in country.

Be informed that I immediately commence the processing of the relevant documents that will facilitate the transfer of the funds into your account with the information you supplied and I will always fax any relevant documents obtained to your secretary. Please instruct your secretary to always deem it fit to acknowledge the receipt of my correspondence as soon as possible.

Meanwhile, it is important to bring to your notice the fact that we are serving Civil Servants who cannot afford any form of exposure considering the nature of this transaction. However, we solicit fervently that you maintain absolute confidentiality on this matter as well as act with despatch on every issue during the course of this *transaction.*

56

Once more, thank you for your anticipated cooperation and confiden⸱ ⸱ ⸱ ⸱ ⸱ ⸱ ⸱ndeavour to call me on phone or send me a fax message on the telephone/fax lines as provided abo

Remember that confidentiality is a key factor to this transaction and ⸱ ⸱ ⸱ ⸱ ⸱ ⸱ep it within realm.

I sincerely wish you a successful business trip to China.

Abu Abubarka.
N.B.   Please, acknowledge this correspondence soonest.

I replied with:

Abu Abubarka,

Hello. I received a phone message from you today, but unfortunately I could not hear it well enough to understand. It would be great if you had e-mail access. I do: bwizard@eoni.com.

I did receive your second fax. Thanks.

All looks good, except for the one line that states, " . . . act with despatch on every issue during the course of this transaction." I'll be up front with you and tell you right now that if any of the issues concern me sending money . . . it won't happen. Why? The possiblity of a 419 scam is always there when dealing with West African countries. I'm not saying you are a 419 scammer, by no means. I just have to be upfront and honest that I don't pay up front fees to anyone for anything. Without that being a concern for you, then, we are still looking good.

Since your phone message was so weak, perhaps faxes would be better, although, as mentioned, e-mail would be best. Cheapest, too.

I await your next communique.

Yours truly,

Brian Wizard

PS: I will be inquiring about machinery via my China contact, as well as my connections in Viet Nam and Thailand. I might as well see what is available in the USA, as well.

*   *   *

"You got another offer for African money?" Martin asked in shock. "I thought they were all poverty stricken."

"They are, hence the scam," I commented. "The count is now over fifty million. Feel free to broaden the spectrum of your dreams."

"To hell with the knife factory!" Martin exclaimed. "I want to call it a day as soon as I get up."

"You've got to keep an interest," I advised him. "I think you'll find that having responsibility for twenty-four hours a day, every day, will be nothing short of work."

"Oh, I have interests," Martin confirmed. "I just don't want to work for a living. I want to work for fun, and live above the poverty level."

"You got it," I praised. "We'll live to work at having fun." I smiled proudly at him as I said, "`Way above the poverty level."

"Damn!" Martin cried. "Wish this weren't a scam."

*   *   *

In a phone conversation with my webmaster I mentioned my Nigerian investigation. She had heard of such scams coming out of Nigeria. "Have you researched the internet to find out how many e-mails are under the name used by this Mohammed guy?" she asked.

"No," I confessed. As a researcher and investigator I needed to become more internet savvy.

"Forward me his name and e-mail address," she instructed. "I'll do some cyber-sleuthing for you. I'll forward anything interesting."

It didn't take long for her to come up with three different addresses for Mo. I drafted a single e-mail destined for them all. Two of the addresses were not familiar to me, either. My curiosity heightened. Who was going to respond?

Mo,

Get in touch with me. We need to talk. Tell David that he is the hero and it is up to him to make this deal work.

Brian Wizard

THIRD and FOURTH CONTACTS

It was the beginning of a new month. I hoped the sense of a new beginning would bring more correspondence from my African family. I felt outside the weird world of the scam without someone working it on me. I wondered if this was a mental conditioning of the scam? Could it be that I had become hypnotized through some subliminal manipulation? Why didn't I call this investigation a waste of time and money? Nothing was what it seemed in the weird world of the scam.

Lethargically, I sat at my computer as it went through its start-up procedure. I knew I'd feel better if one of the addresses for Mo answered my last e-mail. I read the split-second flashes of new e-mails as they downloaded into my computer. Two e-mails from Mo rejuvenated my interest.

I didn't need to open the first e-mail after reading its subject line's announcement of undeliverable e-mail.

I noticed neither e-mail carried Mo's familiar address.

The second e-mail was not from the Mo I had been dealing with. Therefore, it was a *new* address. It was by all accounts a *new Mo*. This one signed the e-mail with the name Abba.

ABACHA DABO MOHAMMED,5/30/00 6:42 AM -0700,Re: Update   **1**

```
X-From_: mohammed.abacha@eudoramail.com  Fri Jan 28 04:13:22 2000
To: bwizard@eoni.com
         Cc:
         Bcc:
X-Attachments:

Attn:- Mr. Brian Wizard.

I have received your e-mails.
```

It is quite unfortunate my elder brother Mr. Mohammed Abacha is been detained along with my late father's chief security officer Major Al- Mustapha while my elder brother has briefed me about the funds and its location were the funds has been logded with a security company in spain.

I am Mr. Abba Abacha the immediate younger brother of Mr. Mohammed Abacha and he has given me the authority and power of attorney to accomplish this deal for him pending the out come of their case with the high court.It is only myself and my elder brother that knows about this funds logded in the vault of a security company in spain.

Myself and my family are under strict security control by the government and we can not travel at all out of Nigeria so you will be given the details of the security company in Spain were the funds is logded in their vault as soon as I hear from you to enable you open up communication on how to arrange and visit the security company to pick up the funds from their vault.

We do not have any connection with the so called David you mentioned in your e-mail, so hence forth stop all further communication with him.

Feel very free to call me on telephone/fax no.:234-1-7745439 only for a very important discussion.

May ALLAH protect and guide us. Awaiting your earliest reply.

Best Regards,

Mr. Abba Abacha.

This e-mail's similarity to the original Mo's initial e-mail amazed me. Its English was better. This character claimed to be the imprisoned Mo's brother. The first Mo claimed to be the imprisoned Mo's son.

"*Spain*" sounded interesting, and a much better place to do business than Benin. I could enjoy going to Spain, scam or no scam. This odd development provided much more potential for a hands-on investigation.

"Hmmm," I hummed in my most inquisitive tone after reading that this new Mo doesn't know David. "How could they not know David?"

It appears I had stirred the bee hive. I thought another kick at the side of the hive might be fun. I drafted this note to the new Mo, Abba.

Mr. Abba Abacha,

You must be familiar with me. I have been assisting your elder brother, Mohammed, in this matter over the past few weeks. You must be familiar with your family lawyer, David Olatunde, as well.

I am familiar with the process presently underway. Please do send me the information regarding the security company in Spain.

Yours truly,
Brian Wizard

I watched my African family grow. It seemed that these different scam factions must not be monitoring each others' prospects. They appeared to be totally independent groups. My guess was, they were all winging it on a roughly drafted outline explaining how to run the scam. If I could, I'd advise them all to become Amway distributors. Such an experience would assist them in their sales pitches and network development skills.

*   *   *

I took my time coming to town the next day. I didn't expect an immediate response from Abba. This guy had to be hungry. He was right on top of his game. His new e-mail was quite interesting.

```
From: "Mohammed K Abacha" <mohammed.abacha@eudoramail.com>
Mime-Version: 1.0
Cc: bwizard@eoni.com
X-Sent-Mail: off
Subject: FW.
X-Sender-Ip: 194.204.195.72
Organization: QUALCOMM Eudora Web-Mail  (http://www.eudoramail.com:80)
Attn:- Mr. Brian Wizard.
```

        I have received your e-mail. Contents carefully understood.
        We do not have a family Lawyer by the name Mr. David Olatunde at all although we have a
family lawyer who ofcourse is a prominent, influencial and moreover a senior Advocate of Nigeria
(SAN).
>My elder brother has been in detention rather you have only discussed with hackers who impersonated
to be my elder brother.
        The details of the security company in Spain is as follows:-

        CONTACT PERSON:- MR. ROGERS PHILIPS.
         NAME OF SECURITY CO.,:- GLOBAL SECURITY S.A.
        DIRECT TEL., NO.:- 34 649 040330.
         FAX NO.:- 34 91 6106046.

        Kindly contact the security company in Spain with the above stated data's immediately.
        Always keep me posted and update me with informations as you progress and discuss with the
security company.
        Awaiting your earliest reply. May ALLAH protect and guide us and save my elder brother from
all the trauma he is going through.

                                Best Regards,
                                Mr. Abba Abacha.

"Hackers! Impersonators!" I shouted in response to what I read. "Who knew?"

I grinned with delight when I read about the contact in Spain. "And the family grows."

With winter bringing me inches of snow daily, I fancied the idea of packing it in to catch some sun on a northern Mediterranean beach. Spain would be in the neighborhood.

Meanwhile, why not have some fun? I decided to call David. I would inform him that the Abacha family considered him to be an impersonating hacker.

With the recorder on, the phone ringing, the butterflies stirred in my belly again.

"Hello," David answered.

"David. Brian Wizard. Have you gone to Benin and picked up the money? Is it in the bank in Cotonou?"

"Oh my god, Mr. Wizard. Where have you been? Why haven't you called me? There is much trouble here. Mohammed is very ill. We must conclude this transaction immediately. Why do you stall? I need . . ."

I knew exactly what David needed, more money. That wasn't the purpose of this call. "There's trouble in the air," I announced. "I was recently e-mailed a note written by Mohammed's brother, Abba. I told him to talk to you. He said he has never heard of you. Do you know him?"

"Mohammed doesn't have a brother named Abba. Abba is a Christian name. Mohammed's family is Muslim. Do not talk to this man any more. He is a fake," David told me.

"A 419 scamster?" I nonchalantly asked.

"Yes. This worries me." David interrogated me. "Did you give him details of our business?"

"No way. That would breach our confidentiality."

"Very good, Mr. Wizard. The money is still in the security vault in Cotonou. When can you go to Cotonou and sign the papers?"

"As soon as I can raise the twenty-five grand Koffie and his people want," I explained as one option. "I don't have it," I explained as a fact. "Can't you borrow it? Doesn't Mohammed have some rich and powerful friends who can help?"

What about my excuse that deferred my requirement of going to Benin? What had happened to the *"humanitarian consideration?"*

Meanwhile, David said, "Mohammed is still in prison, Mr. Wizard. He is not able to contact his rich and powerful friends. They worry that association with the Abacha family might make them enemies of the new government, too."

"Okay, David. I'm still trying to raise the money. You'll have to exercise patience. Meanwhile, try to come up with some money. You have power of attorney to sign all the papers, remember? Koffie is not expecting *m e*. He is expecting *you*," I reminded him. "I'll call again for an update. Good night." I waited to hear David acknowledge that I was hanging up before I disconnected.

"Good night, Mr. Wizard," David said. His voice expressed his disappointment that I was not sending him any money.

"Very interesting," I mused. "The impersonators are calling the impersonators, impersonators."

I then drafted a note to fax to Mr. Roger Philips in Spain.

Global Security. S.A.
Mr. Roger Phillips,
     This letter is designed to initiate communication with you in regards to financial transactions coming to me from Mr. Abba Abacha. Please respond at your soonest convenience so that we can proceed with the transfer of funds presently being held by you for Mr. Abacha. E-mail, or Fax, is the best form of communication.

Yours truly,
Brian Wizard

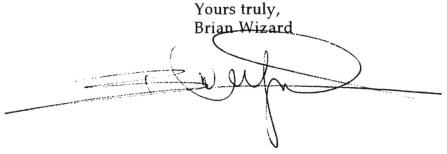

Unfortunately, no one ever picked up the phone, not even a fax machine. I e-mailed Abba, informing him of my difficulty getting through to Spain. I added a postscript: *You have never heard of David Olatunde?*

*   *   *

The new Mo, Abba, came right back at me. I wondered if this guy ever slept. I tried the Spain number again. The fax machine came on. I sent the fax I wrote to Mr. Philips.

ABACHA DABO MOHAMMED, 12/6/99 4:17 AM -0700, Re: Update   1

```
X-From_: abacha_mohammed@eudoramail.com  Mon Dec  6 03:17:42 1999
To: "Brian Wizard" <bwizard@eoni.com>
Date: Mon, 06 Dec 1999 12:17:05 +0100
From: "ABACHA DABO MOHAMMED" <abacha_mohammed@eudoramail.com>
Mime-Version: 1.0
X-Sent-Mail: on
Subject: Re: Update
X-Sender-Ip: 208.243.226.224
Organization: QUALCOMM Eudora Web-Mail  (http://www.eudoramail.com:80)

Attn:- Mr. Brian Wizard.

I have received your e-mail dated 3rd Dec., 1999. Contents well noted.

Mr. David Olatunde is a fake fellow. Did you send any money to the fake fellow? If he has requested
you send him money kindly desist from doing that.
```

If you are finding it difficult to contact Spain always continue to dial untill you will get through successfully.

kindly get back to me immediately you establish contact with Spain for update and make sure furnish m with all the details of your communication with the security company in Spain.

Always call me on telephone/fax no.:- 234-1-7745439 only for a very important discussion by 9.00am to 10.00am your local time.

awaiting your prompt reply.May ALLAH guide and protect us.

Best Regards,

Mr. Abba Abacha.

"Wow!" Abba had come down hard on David.
I replied with:

ABACHA DABO MOHAMMED,5/30/00 6:53 AM -0700,Re: Update   **1**

```
          To: "ABACHA DABO MOHAMMED" <abacha_mohammed@eudoramail.com>
        From: Brian Wizard <bwizard@pop3.eoni.com>
     Subject: Re: Update
          Cc:
         Bcc:
X-Attachments:

Mr. Abacha,
        Yes, I did pay David some money, plus I ended up with quite a large phone bill. A "fake
fellow", you say. That's too bad. I worry not, though, as things have a way of taking care of
themselves. "What you give, you receive," and all that.
        I have just faxed Spain. It took three tries, but it finally went through. Tell me more of
what to expect, if you can.
        There is a storm coming. If I get snowed in it will only be for a couple of days. I'll be in
touch as soon as possible.
        Have you ever heard of the Nigerian Federal Government's Contract Reveiw Committee and Abu
Abubarka?
        I await your next words,
                                Brian Wizard
```

I arrived in town earlier than normal as I had a new and vital under-
taking: the reconstruction of my snowplow. I swung into the post office on
my way to the welding shop. What I found in my post office box was
almost too funny. Someone in Tanzania had decided to forward me yet
another unsolicited business proposal. The letter had taken a month to
travel from Tanzania to my post office box.

DR. EMMA JOHNSON BSC., ICAN, MBA., Ph.D.

EXECUTIVE CHAIRMAN
CONTRACT AWARD COMMITTEE (N.N.P.C)
IKOYI - LAGOS NIGERIA
TEL/FAX: 234-90-405410

NOVEMBER 25, 1999

STRICTLY CONFIDENTIAL

DEAR SIR,

REQUEST FOR URGENT CONFIDENTIAL BUSINESS RELATIONSHIP.
RE: TRANSFER OF US$32 MILLION INTO YOUR ACCOUNT.

AFTER DUE DELIBERATION WITH MY COLLEAGUES, I DECIDED TO FORWARD TO YOU THIS BUSINESS PROPOSAL. WE WANT A RELIABLE PERSON WHO CAN ASSIST US RECEIVE A TRANSFER OF THE SUM OF THIRTY-TWO MILLION U.S. DOLLARS (US$32,000,000.00) INTO HIS/HER BANK ACCOUNT.

THIS FUND RESULTED FROM AN OVER-INVOICED BILL OF A CONTRACT AWARDED BY US TO FOREIGN FIRM UNDER THE FEDERAL BUDGET ALLOCATION. THE PROJECT WAS DULY EXECUTED AND COMMISSIONED, AND THE CONTRACTORS PAID THEIR ACTUAL COST OF THE CONTRACT. WE ARE THEREFORE LEFT WITH A BALANCE OF US$32 MILLION AS THE OVER-INVOICED AMOUNT, WHICH WE NOW WANT TO TRANSFER INTO YOUR ACCOUNT FOR OUR MUTUAL PERSONAL USE. YOUR ASSISTANCE AND SUPPORT IS NEEDED BECAUSE. AS PUBLIC SERVANTS, WE ARE NOT ALLOWED TO OPERATE A FOREIGN BANK ACCOUNT WHERE SUCH MONIES CAN BE HIDDEN UNTIL RETIREMENT. WE PLAN TO USE PARTLY, OUR POSITIONS IN THE GOVERNMENT TO INFLUENCE CERTAIN PROCEDURES TO REALISE OUR TARGET.

WE HAVE AGREED TO SHARE THE PROCEED AS FOLLOWS:
(A)   60% FOR US, (B) 30% FOR YOU (ACCOUNT OWNER), 10% TO REFUND ALL INCIDENTAL EXPENSES INCURRED BY BOTH PARTIES INCLUDING OFFICIAL CHARGES AND BANK TAXES, COST OF TRAVELLING ETC.

AS YOU MAY WANT TO KNOW AND TO MAKE YOU LESS CURIOUS, I GOT YOUR CONTACT FROM THE "WHO IS WHO IN THE WORLD DIRECTORY". PRESENTLY, I AM THE EXECUTIVE CHAIRMAN OF THE CONTRACT TENDER AND AWARD COMMITTEE OF THE NIGERIA NATIONAL PETROLEUM CORPORATION (NNPC). PLEASE BE ASSURED THAT THE BUSINESS IS TOTALLY SAFE, SECURE AND THE SUCCESS GUARANTEED AS IT WAS CAREFULLY PLANNED. WE ARE GOING TO USE OUR POWER, INFLUENCE AND CONNECTIONS IN THE GOVERNMENT TO MAKE IT A HITCH-FREE OPERATION FROM THE BEGINNING TO THE END.

HAVING PUT IN MANY YEARS IN GOVERNMENT SERVICE, WE HAVE BEEN PATIENTLY LOOKING FOR THIS TYPE OF OPPORTUNITY AND HAVING COME NOW, IT IS TO US, A GOLDEN AND LIFE TIME OPPORTUNITY WHICH WE CANNOT AFFORD TO MISS.

IF YOU CAN ASSIST US AND WOULD LIKE TO SHARE IN THE GOD'S GIVEN OPPORTUNITY, PLEASE SEND TO ME BY FAX YOUR BANK DATAS:- (1) BANK ACCOUNT NUMBER, (2) NAME AND ADDRESS OF YOUR BANK, (3) TELEX, TELEPHONE AND FAX NUMBERS OF THE BANK, (4) YOUR OFFICE AND HOME TELEPHONE/FAX NUMBERS FOR EASY AND FASTER COMMUNICATION. YOUR BANK INFORMATION WILL ENABLE US APPLY, PROCESS AND SECURE APPROVALS FROM VARIOUS GOVERNMENT MINISTRIES AND PARASTATALSO CONCERNED. INCLUDING N.N.P.C. AND THE CENTRAL BANK, AFTER WHICH THE FUND WILL BE WIRED STRAIGHT TO YOUR ACCOUNT. I AND MY PARTNER WILL COME TO YOUR COUNTRY THE MOMENT THE FUND IS CONFIRMED IN YOUR ACCOUNT TO RECEIVE OUR SHARE WHICH WILL BE PLOUGHED BACK INTO INVESTMENT AND IMPORTATION FROM YOUR COMPANY/COUNTRY. BEFORE THIS, YOU MAY BE REQUIRED BY THE CENTRAL BANK OF NIGERIA TO COME AND SIGN THE FINAL PAYMENT RELEASE ORDER (F.P.R.O.) AUTHORIZING THEM FINALLY TO TRANSFER THE MONEY TO YOUR A/C.

THIS TRANSACTION IS THOUGH, 100% SAFE AND SECURE, BUT THE INFORMATION HIGHLY SENSITIVE, YOU ARE ADVISED TO KEEP IT STRICTLY PRIVATE AND CONFIDENTIAL. YOU MUST NOT DISCUSS IT WITH A THIRD PARTY, EVEN YOUR BANKER UNTIL EVERYTHING IS COMPLETED HERE. YOU MUST DISPLAY HIGH LEVEL OF MATURITY, UNDERSTANDING AND CONFIDENTIALITY AND EXTEND YOUR MAXIMUM SUPPORT AND CO-OPERATION TO US, WHILE OUR GUIDING PRINCIPLE IN THIS RELATIONSHIP SHALL BE MUTUAL TRUST, HONESTY AND RELIABILITY. PLEASE LET YOUR COMMUNICATION BE THROUGH FAX AND TELEPHONE ONLY. YOUR URGENT REPLY TO FAX/TEL NUMBERS: 234-90-405410 WILL BE APPRECIATED.

BEST REGARDS,

DR. EMMA JOHNSON

As usual, I verbalized my comments as I read along.
"Emma, talk to me, girl," I said enthusiastically. I assumed the name Emma denoted a female correspondent. Emma was the first of her gender

in my growing African family. That made her a certified resident of the weird world of the scam.

"Another thirty-two million! Wait till the boys hear this!" I expressed my joy. That made the count $82,320,000. That was not counting the $475,000,000 David said he had to filter into my account in $25,000,000 increments. The entire total was $557,320,000. My twenty-five percent was looking mighty fine.

I especially liked what I read in the last part of Emma's fax. *"THIS TRANSACTION IS THOUGH, 100% SAFE AND SECURE."* I re-read the typo and decided Emma meant, "thoroughly."

Then came the part of the scam that was my responsibility: my personal fabrication of the truth. Again, let me explain myself. I am a novelist, not a priest. So, I lied. My rationalization was: Everything I'm being told is a lie. Therefore, lies are our mutual cache of weapons and ammunition. That is a rule of the game. Without lies, scams can't exist.

Being a veteran of such business proposals, I fired off this congratulatory note to Emma, including my banking particulars.

Brian Wizard
P.O.Box 42
Wallowa, Or. 97885 USA
541 886 0119 (tele/fax)

December 8, 1999

Ms. Emma Johnson,

Congratulations for enlisting my talent in your quest for an entrepreneurial partner. You have selected well.

Now, above and below are the details you requested in order to transfer the 32 million US dollars.

I'm sure you have the talent and arrangement to pay all fees and make all the details stamped, signed, notarized, etc. without my assistance. Of course, you have my permission to extract from the funds all relative fees.

I will monitor the bank account for the deposit.

I do hope to find us working partners in the near future. SEND THE MONEY! We'll do God's bidding with our rewards.

Yours truly,

Brian Wizard

Bank Account Details:

Klamath First Federal
106 S.W. First St.
Enterprise, Or. 97828
Phone: USA 541 426 3124
Fax: 541 426 4747

Routing Number, including account number: 323 270 300   48 70043751
Name of Beneficiary: Brian Wizard

WARNING! Be wary of the imfamous Nigerian 419 scam.

I even tipped my hand concerning my knowledge of the Nigerian 419 Scam. What reaction would that remark stimulate?

On a recent trip to my bank I had informed the teller that I expected a large influx of capital into my account. "Twenty-five million, or more."

"I'll drop dead to the floor," the teller remarked.

I thought I should bring her a pillow the next time I saw her and informed her of yet another source of big money.

*   *   *

For next three days the only communication I had from my African friends was silence. No news was good news? Maybe. I needed something to hold onto, so I dropped Abba a quick e-mail.

Mohammed K Abacha,5/30/00 7:11 AM -0700,Re: update. 1

```
      To: "Mohammed K Abacha" <mabacha@eudoramail.com>
    From: Brian Wizard <bwizard@pop3.eoni.com>
 Subject: Re: update.
      Cc:
     Bcc:
X-Attachments:

Abba,
        So, what's up with the transactions? I can't move until I know for sure that everyone is in
place and ready for me. I am looking for a happy ending to this saga. I need to know when I should
move, where to go, who to meet and what you plan on doing after this transaction(s) has been
completed.
                      Fill me in on the details.
                      Brian Wizard
```

The next day, I received this e-mail in reply:

ABACHA DABO MOHAMMED, 12/13/99 8:38 AM -0700, Re: Update

```
X-From_: abacha_mohammed@eudoramail.com  Mon Dec 13 07:39:11 1999
To: "Brian Wizard" <bwizard@eoni.com>
Date: Mon, 13 Dec 1999 16:38:24 +0100
From: "ABACHA DABO MOHAMMED" <abacha_mohammed@eudoramail.com>
Mime-Version: 1.0
X-Sent-Mail: on
Subject: Re: Update
X-Sender-Ip: 208.243.226.224
Organization: QUALCOMM Eudora Web-Mail  (http://www.eudoramail.com:80)

ATTN:- MR. BRIAN WIZARD.

I HAVE RECEIVED YOUR BOTH E-MAILS.

YOU SHOULD EXERCISE A LITTLE PATIENCE AND WAIT FOR UPDATE FROM SPAIN. KEEP ME POSTED AND ALWAYS UPDATE
ME WITH THE PROGRESSIVE REPORT AS YOU DISCUSS WITH SPAIN.

AWAITING YOUR EARLIEST REPLY.

BEST REGARDS,

MR. ABBA ABACHA.
```

I replied:

ABACHA DABO MOHAMMED, 12/13/99 1:27 PM +0100, Re: Update

```
       To: "ABACHA DABO MOHAMMED" <abacha_mohammed@eudoramail.com>
     From: Brian Wizard <bwizard@eoni.com>
  Subject: Re: Update
       Cc:
      Bcc:
X-Attachments:

I sit, I wait.   Brian Wizard

PS: Do you know of Emma Johnson? She too is a Nigerian Contracter. She has 32 million to send my way.
Along with Mohammed, ( your brother, or a fake) and David, who have 500 million to send my way, there
is Abu Abubakar and his 25 million. Then there's you. Wow!
```

If Abba thought David and the first Mo were fake fellows, what would
he have to say about Emma and Abu?

*   *   *

On my next visit to the office I found out what Abba thought of Emma
and Abu.

```
X-From_: abacha_mohammed@eudoramail.com  Wed Dec 15 04:21:49 1999
To: "Brian Wizard" <bwizard@eoni.com>
Date: Wed, 15 Dec 1999 13:20:57 +0100
From: "ABACHA DABO MOHAMMED" <abacha_mohammed@eudoramail.com>
Mime-Version: 1.0
X-Sent-Mail: on
X-Expiredinmiddle: true
Subject: Re: Update
X-Sender-Ip: 208.243.226.224
Organization: QUALCOMM Eudora Web-Mail  (http://www.eudoramail.com:80)
```

ATTN:- MR. BRIAN WIZARD.

I HAVE RECEIVED YOUR E-MAIL OF 13TH DEC., 1999 WITH THANKS.

AFTER A CAREFUL INVESTIGATION THAT HAS BEEN CONDUCTED MESSERS EMMA JOHNSON, COHORTS DAVID AND ABU ABUBARKAR WHO OFCOURSE HASN'T A CENT TO TRANSFER TO YOU AND ARE NOT IN THE POSITION TO INFLUENCE THE TRANSFER OF A DOLLAR RATHER ALL THEIR PROPOSALS TO YOU VARYING FROM THE SUM OF US332,000,000.00, US$500,000,000.00 AND US$25,320,000.00 ARE ALL FAKE AND FALSE. HOWEVER EMMA JOHNSON TOLD YOU ABOUT TRANSFERRING MONEY WITH MY ELDER BROTHER MOHAMMED ABACHA WHO IS CURRENTLY IN DETENTION WITH THE CHIEF SECURITY OFFICER OF MY LATE FATHER MAJOR HAMZA AL MUSTAPHA WITH TWO OTHERS AND OFCOURSE THEY APPEARED BEFORE THE HIGH COURT ON 13TH DEC., 1999 AND THEY ARE STILL IN REMAND WITHOUT OPTION OF BAIL. THIS IS QUITE INCREDIBLE AND OUTRAGEOUS.

IF YOU WISH TO PAY ME A VISIT YOU ARE WELCOME WITH THE SHOWING OF SIGHT, ENTERTAINMENT, GOOD FOOD AND LOTS OF FUN AS YOU DESIRE.

AWAITING YOUR EARLIEST REPLY. MAY ALLAH GUIDE, PROTECT AND LEAD US INTO THE NEW YEAR 2000 (MILLENIUM). WISHING YOU A HAPPY CHRISTMAS AND NEW YEAR IN ADVANCE.

BEST REGARDS,

MR. ABBA ABACHA.

"Yo!" Martin called out, as he entered my office. "How's things going in the weird world of the scam?"

"Everyone claims everyone else is a fake. Ironically, they're all right." I laughed. "They are all fakes. Including me!"

"What's the count up to today?" Martin asked. "Any new money come in?"

"The new guy isn't talking numbers, so the total remains the same, only five hundred-plus million and change."

"Let me know when it hits a billion. I've never met a billionaire before," Martin confessed.

"We can only hope."

"If it wasn't for hope, you'd be out of an investigation," Martin reminded me.

I decided to send this e-mail to Abba, hoping to get a rise out of him about the 419 scam aspect of his life.   69

ABACHA DABO MOHAMMED,12/7/99 5:51 PM +0100,Re: Update

```
        To: "ABACHA DABO MOHAMMED" <abacha_mohammed@eudoramail.com>
      From: Brian Wizard <bwizard@eoni.com>
   Subject: Re: Update
        Cc:
       Bcc:
X-Attachments:
```

Mr. Abacha,
        Thanks for the advice. I hate chasing my shadow, nor do I like having my time wasted. I
patiently await word from Spain. Now, tell me this, if you would, please: what is the plan?
        As you can see from my past experiences, I have experienced the famous Nigerian 419 scam.
Can you asure me your plan isn't going to waste my time, or have me chasing my shadow? I hope so. I'd
like a happy moment to come from all this.
        I will be gone until Friday. On my return I should have something from Spain. I'll contact
you then.
        Take care. Brian Wizard

                              *   *   *

   I entered my office around ten the next morning. The fog was not only
thick, but frozen over everything. All things outdoors wore a three-eighths
inch ice coat. The physical world looked more like a film negative than the
real thing. My real world looked as surreal as the weird world of the scam
felt.
   My office was warm. I had heard the prediction of Arctic air. In prepa-
ration, I had turned up the heat. Upon my entrance I sighed in relief,
"Ahhh." A fax lay rolled up in front of the machine. I could only hope it was
from the good doctor Emma. It was.

DR. EMMA JOHNSON BSC.. ICAN.. MBA..Ph.D.

90

EXECUTIVE CHAIRMAN

CONTRACT AWARD COMMITTEE (N.N.P.C)

IKOYI – LAGOS NIGERIA

TEL/FAX: 234-90-405410

December 21, 1999.

To: **Brian Wizard**
      USA

fax: 007-1-541-8860119

Dear Sir,

I refer to your fax dated Dec. 8, 1999 and wish to thank you for your prompt positive action.

The bank account particulars have been noted.

Meanwhile everything looks fine- I and my colleague have tasked ourselves to raise some fund needed for running the project; all the material and human resources needed put in place, and application for the payment filed today.

The only problem I can say, is the usual bureaucratic red tapes and the snail speed of doings in the Government establishments here, especially to obtain approvals for huge sum of money.
However, I am pleased to let you know that I have been able to organise some powerful guys in the system whom we are going to use to realise the deal quickly.

Actually, they have promised to co-operate with us but an insider who is very close to them, has just advised that I try and buy them some nice gift to commit them strongly and win their hearts proper. Anyhow, I will try to find out what items would be most interesting to them and shall advise you accordingly in due time. I would request that you procure the gift item and send down to me for presentation. With this working plan, I am sure, by the grace of God, we will secure all the necessary approvals for the payment within a very short time- say 7 days. In the meantime, I shall keep you informed of the day to day progress.

Finally, I want to remind you to continue to keep and maintain the confidentiality of the transaction.
I am highly placed in the government and with my reputation and family background, I cannot afford to be mentioned in a scandal. That is the reason why we planned this deal to be watertight, 100% safe and secured. Equally, I cannot afford to miss this deal which I have planned to use the proceed to finance my political ambition in the very near future. I want to believe that you are equally a man of honour and responsibility who would not like messed up. So let us be reserved, very secretive and calm, even to the bankers until every process is completed at this end and the fund is ready for transfer to your account. Above all, we must operate and remain as one body and one soul in love, mutual trust and belief in God to see us through. Amen.

Please reply to confirm receipt.

Best regards,

Dr. Emma Johnson.

She was obviously undaunted by my mention of the scam. She was shameless.

I will admit, I liked reading the information contained in the fax. I actually liked these people. I had to respect their personal and professional dedication to the scam. I could see how some had grown, no doubt through practice, and were upwardly mobile on the ladder of the Ultimate Scam.

I spoke as I read. *"The bank account particulars have been noted."* That was a good sign that they were keeping track.

"Things are looking good." I praised the good doctor for her diligence in raising funds.

Uh oh! *". . . buy gifts for them."* I felt hit by a psychological sucker punch. I should have seen it coming.

My heart froze in place for a second when I read the part about me being an equally honorable and responsible man who would not like *"messed up."* In my best Robert DeNiro impression, I asked, "You talking to me? You *talking* to *me*?" Mess what up? My reputation? Ha ha ha ha! You'd have to get up pretty early in the morning to beat me at that game. Mess me up personally? I let my impression of Dirty Harry ask, "You feeling lucky, punk?"

"Hey-hey!" I cheered, feeling my spirit lifted by the sermon delivered in the last paragraph: "...*we must operate and remain as one body and one soul in love, mutual trust and belief in God* ..."

Somebody had done some time in California and read the small print on a bottle of Dr. Bronner's 100% Castile Soap. "'We are 'All-One-God.' Amen, my friends." I accented my concurrence with my palms pressed together in prayer.

*　*　*

Dr. Emma's last fax didn't give me any instructions to follow. I casually rode along in the family boat as it sailed across the sea of life in the weird world of the scam. I enjoyed a constant sense of light expectation. I had confidence that the ball of opportunity was rolling in my direction. The true reward of that opportunity was yet to become known. For the moment, all I wanted was more action.

My request materialized two days later in the form of two more faxes:

NIGERIAN NATIONAL PETROLEUM CORPORATION
7, Kofo Abayomi Street, Victoria Island - Lagos.

Ref: *NNPC/FGN/VOL. 001-99*

Cublegram: NAPETCOR

Date: *December 23, 1999*

From: **ENGINEER DONALD ESONG**
Director Contract Allocation Department
Nigeria National Petroleum Corporation (NNPC)

ATTN: **BRIAN WIZARD**
USA

Dear Sir,

APPROVAL NOTICE ON CONTRACT NO. NNPC/PED/2021-D: 97 FOR USD 32 MILLION(THIRTY TWO MILLION UNITED STATES DOLLARS)

We received previously an application for approval and transfer of your contract fund of thirty two million U.S. Dollars.

In view of the terms of the contract, your application has been granted and payment recommended to the Minister of Finance, Abuja for foreign exchange allocation approval; the Governor-Central bank of Nigeria, CBN and other appropriate authorities for quick disposal of your contract payment.

Attached herewith is a copy of the approved document from (NNPC) in favour of beneficiaries, including BRIAN WIZARD

So, you should look forward subsequently to receiving further instructions from the office of the Ministry of Finance and the Central bank of Nigeria, CBN for your transfer.

In the meantime accept our congratulations.

Regards

Engr. Donald Esong

12-23-1999 08:23PM

NIGERIAN NATIONAL PETROLEUM CORPORATION
7, Kofo Abayomi Street, Victoria Island - Lagos.

APPROVED FOR PAYMENT

Ref: NNPC/FGN/VOL. 001/99
Date: *NOVEMBER 23, 1999*

Cublegram: NAPETCOR
TO: THE HONOURABLE MINISTER
FEDERAL MINISTRY OF FINANCE
FEDERAL SECRETARIAT, IKOYI
LAGOS.

DEAR SIR,

APPLICATION FOR FOREIGN EXCHANGE APPROVAL

THIS IS TO CERTIFY THAT THE UNDERLISTED COMPANIES HAVE COMPLETED THEIR VARIOUS PROJECTS WITH THE NIGERIAN NATIONAL PETROLEUM CORPORATION, NNPC.

HAVING SATISFACTORILY EXECUTED THE PROJECTS AND THE ORIGINAL CERTIFICATE OF COMPLETION DULY ISSUED, WE HEREBY APPLY FOR EXCHANGE CONTROL APPROVAL IN THEIR FAVOUR TO ENABLE US COMPLETE OUR PART OF THE CONTRACT AGREEMENT.

THE BENEFICIARIES ARE:

1. **SYSTEM TEC, INC**
USA

/ ... MR. KOPEL HERD

AMOUNT: US$ 54,600,400

COMPANY / BENEFICIARY
2. **BRIAN WIZARD**
P.O. BOX 42, WALLOWA,
OR. 97885 USA

ATTN: BRIAN WIZARD

AMOUNT: US$32,000,000.00

COMPANY / BENEFICIARY
3. **EXXON OIL, INC**
ATTN: MR. RON WARREN
USA

BANK PARTICULARS

AMERICAN EXPRESS BANK NEW YORK
A/C NO: 009-010-00014-6
A/C NAME: SYSTEM TEC INC.
PURPOSE OF PAYMENT: NNPC CONTRACT NO:
NNPC/PED/185:98

BANK PARTICULARS
KLAMATH FIRST FEDERAL
106 S.W. FIRST ST., ENTERPRISE, OR. 97828
TEL: 541-426-3124, FAX: 541-426-4747
A/C NO: 487004375
ROUTING NO: 323270300

A/C NAME: BRIAN WIZARD

PURPOSE OF PAYMENT NNPC CONTRACT NO:
NNPC/PED/2021/D:97

CREDIT SUSSIE
GENEVA
BRANCH NO: 2001
A/C NAME: EXXON SERVICES
ATTN: MR. T.A. SCHWARTZ.
A/C NO: 0008126345

NNPC Sign

AMOUNT: US$83,050,000

PLEASE ADVISE CBN ACCORDINGLY.

THANKING YOU FOR USUAL CO-OPERATION.

WE REMAIN.

YOURS FAITHFULLY.
N. N. P. C.
MR. GRACE UBA
CHIEF ACCOUNTANT LAGOS
NIGERIAN NATIONAL PETROLEUM
CORPORATION (NNPC) LAGOS.

PURPOSE OF PAYMENT
NNPC/EED/26:R96
*ACCOUNT TO BE DEBITED:
NNPC-FEDERATION A/C WITH CBN NO.230237 FGN

NIGERIAN NATIONAL PETROLEUM CORPORATION
DESPATCHED
SIGN ... DATE 23-12-

What amazed me in my reading of the fax from Dr. Emma's colleague, Donald Esong, was the name of a notorious culprit of the Nigerian Scam being the party she represented. The Nigerian National Petroleum Corporation. I had read the petroleum company's name in a report published on the internet by the 419 Coalition.

"APPROVED FOR PAYMENT!" I liked reading that. I had more signatures, stamps, and seals confirming the soon-to-take-place transfer of thirty-two million dollars into my account.

Again, just for fun, I did the math;

$$\begin{array}{r} 500,000,000 \\ 25,320,000 \\ \underline{32,000,000} \\ 557,320,000 \text{ BIG BUCKS!} \end{array}$$

My cut at 25% = $20,580,000

"Damn!" I said in mimic of Martin's delivery of disappointment. "Wish this weren't a scam."

After reading the bottom of the first page I understood that *". . . further instructions from the Ministry of Finance and the Central Bank of Nigeria . . . for transfer . . ."* were coming.

"Congratulations accepted," was my final remark.

*   *   *

As usual, the commercial craze of the Holidaze Season inevitably brought most business activities to a halt. I sat back and waited, somewhat anxiously, for the season of feigned well-wishing to expire. I know that sounded very humbugish. Unfortunately, for the most part I find it to be true. If you don't have it in you to wish joy and happiness to the world and goodwill towards all people 24/7- forever, then you truly don't have it for a few weeks out of the year.

Right after the holidaze I faxed Abu a note, hoping to stir him out of early retirement from the scam:

Abu Abubarka,
    It would be a good time to get in touch with me now. Do so by fax or e-mail.
    Thanks, Brian Wizard

PS: I have listened to your last phone message, weeks old now, many times before and after my return, but still it is too weak to understand. I think it said you were sending two faxes, or two packages. I received neither.

*   *   *

Finally, the silence broke on the last day of the year. I found multiple faxes rolled up in a pile at the base of my fax machine. The good doctor had been working hard. With the happiness and joy recently expressed by all the lucky children of the world who had been good all year, I opened the rolled up fax sheets as if each one were a present from Santa Claus himself.

FEDERAL MINISTRY OF FINANCE
FEDERAL SECRETARIAT BUILDING
IKOYI - LAGOS, NIGERIA

NO: FGN/FMF/FX/1642/99

CERTIFICATE OF FOREIGN EXCHANGE
ALLOCATIONFOREX DISKETTE 11/001/99

This is to certify that the Federal Ministry of Finance has approved ans allocated in Foreign Currency the underlisted payment:-

Foreign Exchange Control Allocation Number:...................... FX-2106: 99

.... NNPC/PED/2021-D: 97

Amount is Foreign Currency:....................... (US$ 32,000,000.00)

.... THIRTY-TWO MILLION U.S. DOLLARS

Beneficiary:....................... BRIAN WIZARD

.... P.O. BOX 42, WALLOWA, OR 97885 USA.

Purpose of Payment:....................... NNPC OFFSHORE CONTRACT

Ref:....................... NNPC/PED/2021-D: 97

Certified by the authority of

SIGN:...........
DATE:...........

ALHAJI ISMAILA USMAN
Federal Ministry of Finance Lagos, Nigeria

Given under my hand on

December 27, 1999

Of course, throughout the excitement I made verbal comments as I read my gifts.

"*Control Allocation Number . . .*" My imagination ran wild for a moment as I read my new secret code name: *FX-2106:99.*

"Beneficiary: Brian Wizard." That looked good. All documents carried official signatures, stamps, and seals of the officials of the Nigerian government. I was on a roll.

I read the next four documents with just as much glee.

FEDERAL MINISTRY OF FINANCE
EXCHANGE CONTROL DIVISION
FEDERAL SECRETARIAT
P. M. B 7207, IKOYI - LAGOS, NIGERIA

Ref No: FMF / ECD / X986 / 99  Date: Dec. 27, 1999

Nigerian National Petroleum Corporation, NNPC
7, Kofo Abayomi Street,
Victoria Island, Lagos.

FEDERAL MINISTRY OF FINANCE
APPROVED FOR PAYMENT

ATTN: BRIAN WIZARD

Dear Sir,

RE: CONFIRMATION OF FOREIGN EXCHANGE APPROVAL ORDER

Reference your application dated December 23, 1999 we confirm the approval, by the Honourable Minister, of One Hundred and Ninety Three Million Six Hundred and Fifty Thousand Four Hundred (193,650,400.00) U.S. Dollars Foreign Exchange allocation as follows:-

1.	SYSTEMTEC, INC USA	USD54,600,400.00
2.	BRIAN WIZARD USA	USD32,000,000.00
3.	EXXON OIL, INC USA	USD83,050,000.00
	TOTAL	USD169,650,400.00

Note that this approval has been forwarded to the Central Bank of Nigeria for further action.

You are expected to notify us when all matters are regularised and cleared.

Regards,

Alhaji Zonkwa Abubarkar
Director General / Federal Ministry of Finance

FEDERAL MINISTRY OF FINANCE
Foreign Exchange Department
CHECKED & APPROVED
Sign............ Date. 27/12/99

Attachments: Certificate of Foreign Exchange allocation for each beneficiary.

cc: *The Presidency - Abuja*
cc: *The Governor - Central Bank of Nigerian*

FEDERAL MINISTRY OF FINANCE
EXCHANGE CONTROL DIVISION
FEDERAL SECRETARIAT
P. M. B 7207, IKOYI - LAGOS, NIGERIA

Ref No: FMF / CBN / X986 / 99

Date: 28 December, 1999

TO: CENTRAL BANK OF NIGERIA
DEBT MANAGEMENT DEPT.
FOREIGN OPERATIONS
TINUBU SQUARE
LAGOS.

ATTN: **BRIAN WIZARD**

DEAR SIR,

CONFIRMATION OF FOREIGN EXCHANGE APPROVAL ORDER

WE HEREBY CONFIRM THE EXCHANGE CONTROL ORDER ON CONTRAC NO.: NNPC/PED/2021-D:97 IN FAVOUR OF:
MR. BOBBY SHARMA, NEW ZEALAND.

SERIAL NO	AMOUNT APPROVED	DATE OF APPROVAL	FILE REK NO.	APPLICANT	BENEFICIARY
XXB132	US$ 32,000,000.00	23-12-99	NNPC/PED/ 2021-D.9 FMF009	NIGERIAN NATIONAL PETROLEUM CORPORATION	BRIAN WIZARD P. O.BOX 42, WALLOWA OR.97885 USA.
AMOUNT IN WORDS:	THIRTY-TWO MILLION UNITED STATES DOLLARS ONLY				
BANKERS:	KLAMATH FIRST FEDERAL 106 S. W. FIRST ST., ENTERPRISE, OR 97828 USA.				

ACCOUNT NO: 487004375

Alhaji Zonkwa Abubarkar

Director General / Federal Ministry of Finance

cc: *The Presidency - Abuja*
cc: *The Nigerian National Petroleum Corporation, NNPC*

FEDERAL MINISTRY OF FINANCE
EXCHANCE CONTROL DIVISION
FEDERAL SECRETARIAT
P. M. B 7207, IKOYI - LAGOS, NIGERIA

Ref No: FMF/AGF/X986/99 ....

Date: Dec. 29, 1999 ....

TO: Accountant-General of the Federation
Federal Republic of Nigeria
Office Complex-Garki
F.C.T., Abuja.

Sir,

EXCHANGE CONTROL APPROVAL ORDER

This Exchange Control Approval Order is in favour of: **BRIAN WIZARD P.O. BOX 42, WALLOWA, USA.** for the amount of **US$32,000,000.00 (Thirty-Two Million United States Dollars only)** payable to: **KLAMATH FIRST FEDERAL 106, S.W. FIRST ST., ENTERPRISE, OR 97828, USA. ACCOUNT NO: 487004375**

The Foreign Exchange Control approval slip and Foreign Payment Approval Order has been sent to Foreign Operations Department, Central Bank of Nigeria, Tinubu Square, Lagos.

Please you are advised to send your payment order to the International Remittance Office of the Central Bank of Nigeria, Tinubu Square, Lagos for clearance, regularisation and transfer.

Yours faithfully,

Alhaji Zonkwa Abubarkar

D/G Fed. Min. of Finance

cc: *The Presidency - Abuja*

CENTRAL BANK OF NIGERIA

DEPARTMENT OF DEBT MANAGEMENT
TINUBU SQUARE, LAGOS
DIRECT FAX LINE: 234-1-7595652

Date: *30th Dec. 1999*

Ref: *CBN/FGN:021-VOL.4*

From the desk of: **M.M.Sani**

Deputy - Governor

Central Bank of Nigeria

Fax: 234-1-7595052

To: Federal Ministry of Finance
        Federal Secretariat, Ikoyi,
        Lagos.

FOR THE ATTENTION OF ALHAJI ABUBARKAR ZONKWA

Dear Sir,

RE: FOREIGN EXCHANGE ALLOCATION NO: FX-2106;99

We refer to your letters dated December 28 1999 respectively, and wish to acknowledge the FOREX ALLO-CATION ORDER for offshore contract payment to messrs SYSTEMTEC INC, USA, BRIAN WIZARD, P.O.BOX42, WALLOWA, OR 97885 USA. and EXXON OIL, INC USA.

Incidentally, the Order is receiving due attention at the top to comply with the stipulated regulations. The transfer will be effected as soon as the beneficiaries are able to complete all the necessary procedures as required.

Beneficiaries shall be advised accordingly in due time.

Best Regards,

Dr. Mohammed M. Sani
Deputy-Governor
CBN

"Confirmation galore," I commented. "Hey, what's this?" I asked, after I noticed a difference between the three beneficiaries listed. "How come Systemtec, Inc. gets fifty-four million and some, and Exxon is approved for eighty-three million and change, and I'm the low man on the payroll with a meager thirty-two million?

"Who is this Bobby Sharma of New Zealand? Perhaps I should give the boy a call?"

I read the continued reports of my having been *Checked and Approved."*

Finally, I found my next instructions: *The transfer will be effected as soon as the beneficiaries are able to complete all the necessary procedures as required.*

Beneficiaries shall be advised accordingly in due time.

Best regards, Dr. Mohammed M. Sani.

I contemplated calling the Central Bank of Nigeria and asking for Dr. Sani.

But first I needed a quick look at the latest e-mail. I found a note from Abba. The first thing I noticed was that his title changed from ABACHA DABO MOHAMMED, with an e-mail address of: abacha-mohammed@eudoramail.com, to Mohammed K Abacha, with an e-mail address of mabacha@eudoramail.com. It read.

Mohammed K Abacha,12/31/99 12:53 PM -0700,HAPPY NEW YEAR.   1

```
X-From_: mabacha@eudoramail.com  Fri Dec 31 11:54:10 1999
To: bwizard@eoni.com
Date: Fri, 31 Dec 1999 11:53:26 -0800
From: "Mohammed K Abacha" <mabacha@eudoramail.com>
Mime-Version: 1.0
Cc: bwizard@eoni.com
X-Sent-Mail: off
X-Expiredinmiddle: true
Subject: HAPPY NEW YEAR.
X-Sender-Ip: 194.204.253.197
Organization: QUALCOMM Eudora Web-Mail  (http://www.eudoramail.com:80)



ATTN:-Mr.BRIAN WIZARD.

HAPPY NEW YEAR.
```

I THANK YOU VERY MUCH FOR YOUR ANSWER ,AND I COMMEND YOUR EFFORTS TOWARD THE REALIZATION OF OUR GOAL
BUT I TOLD YOU THAT MY ELDER BROTHER MR.MOHAMMED ABACHA HAS GIVEN ME ,THE FULL AUTHORITY AND POWER OF
ATTORNEY TO ACCOMPLISH THIS DEAL FOR HIM ,PENDING THE OUT COME OF THEIR CASE WITH THE HIGH COURT , AND
HE TOLD ME TO REPLY ALL E-MAILS ,AND A LETTERS FROM OUR ASSOCIATES ABROAD AND HE INSTRUCTED ME TO SEND
TEST QUESTIONS FOR ANYBODY SAID THAT THERE IS A BUSINESS WITH MR.MOHAMMED ABACHA , I AM AWARE THAT
THERE ARE A PERSONS IMPERSONATED OUR ASSOCIATES ABROAD ,SO MY BROTHER ADVICE ME TO BE CAREFUL SO YOU
SHOULD ANSWER ALL MY QUESTIONS , BEFORE WE CAN CARRY ON FOR THE CONCLUSION THIS BUSINESS AND IF YOU
ANSWER ALL QUESTIONS THEN WE CAN SEND YOU MONEY THROUGH OUR FOREIGN ACCOUNTS TO COVER THE BILLS ,
MOREOVER WE CAN SEND YOU THE TELEPHONES NUMBERS FOR OUR ASSOCIATES ABROAD AND WE CAN MAKE WITH YOU
OTHER TRANSACTIONS AND INVESTMENTS ABROAD .

WE HAVE LOST OUR POWER ,MOST OF OUR FRIENDS ,OUR PASSPORTS THE SOLDIERS WHO ONCE PROTECTED US NOW KEEP
WATCH ON US , CHECKING CARS THAT COME INTO THE COMPOUND AND FOLLOWING FAMILY MEMBERS WHEN WE GO OUT ,
WE ARE WAITING FOR OUR FREEDOM AND OUR FORTUNE.

THESE IS QUESTIONS FOR YOU :
1)-WHAT IS THE PASS WORD ?.
2)-WHAT IS THE BAGGAGE N0 ?.
3)-WHAT IS THE NAME OF SECURITY COMPANY ?.
4)-WHAT IS THE COUNTRY OF SECURITY COMPANY
   LOCATE ? .
5)-WHAT IS THE NAME OF OUR ATTORNEY ?.
6)-HOW MUCH ARE YOU AWARE THAT WAS CONTAINED IN   THE BOXES ?.
7)-AMOUNT CHARGE PER DAY FOR THE BOXES IS IT
   10$,50$,100$,200$,OR FREE OF CHARGE ?.
8)-HAVE YOU BEEN MET OUR ATTORNEY ?.
   IF YES SPECIFY WHEN(DATE),WHERE(COUNTRY).
9)-HAS BOXES BEEN REGISTERED UNDER YOUR NAME OR   OTHER ...SPECIFY THE NAMES EXACTLY ?.
10)-HAVE YOU BEEN VISIT NIGERIA BEFORE ?.
11)-HAVE YOU BEEN VISIT THIS COUNTRY
    (IVORY COAST,GANA,SOUTH AFRICA ,ENGLAND,
    SWIZARLAND,DENEMRK,HOLLAND,GERMNY)IN
    RESPECT OF THIS BUSINESS ?.
12)-HAVE YOU BEEN MET OUR ASSOCIATES ABROAD ?.
    IF YES WRITE THEIR NAMES .
13)-SEND ME A COPY OF YOUR DOCUMENTS .
    A/-A COPY OF OWNERSHIP CERTIFICATE.
    B/-A COPY OF PAPERWORK.
    C/-A COPY OF PAPERS STATING.

NOTE THAT YOU SHOULD TRY TO SCAN ABOVE DOCUMENTS
AND SEND IT VIA E-MAIL ATTACHMENT ,DO QUICKLY FOR FURTHER DELAYS ON THIS BUSINESS IS UNFAVOURABLE TO
BOTH US .

YOURS SINCERELY .

The message itself I found somewhat weird, if not disturbing. The first
part was fine. The Nigerian press verified all this information. The test
questions were a bit much. I didn't like them, so I replied with:

Abba,

I can't answer your test questions. Such answers would breach my promise of confidentiality. Sorry. If you don't know enough about me already, then I can only imagine that you are not who you say you are, and this e-mail is a hoax.

Also, I don't have a scanner, so I can't e-mail you any documents. In addition, for confidentiality reasons, I wouldn't do that.

Yours truly,
Brian Wizard

*   *   *

Communications fell silent for a few days. Then a fax came in from Dr. Emma.

From:	Emma Johnson	4th Dec. 2000
	Lagos - Nigeria.	
Tel/Fax:	234-90-405410	

Dear Sir,

I and my wife are happy to send to you and your family some good wishes of long life, good health, love and happiness and prosperity in this new year and even beyond. I am more than happy also to announce to you today, that our transaction has recorded some tremendous success.

You know, we have tirelessly been on this project, to secure all the necessary approvals from the goernment quarters. Our effort has yielded result culminating onto securing approvals for the payment which I attach herewith for your reference.

It was not an easy fight at all, because we did not take any rest during the Xmas and New Year break, but I thank God so much that today we have come out of it successfully.

My Lawyer applied on our behalf for copies of the transaction/ approvals to be released to us. Please understand that the documents are very sensitive and confidential financial papers made for the government consumption only.

You are advised to treat them so and never to release any part of it to a third party, until everything is completed at this end, and the fund is ready to leave to your account. I should advise also that you do not release them to your bankers until the confirmation of the fund in your account. I hope you would understand please. Take note that we are now at the last lap of the transaction, that is, within the Central Bank system and being the bonafide beneficary of the fund, central bank of Nigeria, CBN, for security reason would be dealing with you directly, henceforth. Therefore, you must always contact me first the moment you receive any information from them.

Remember I mentioned to you earlier about the need to present some gifts to some of the top offcials, unfortunately you have not responded positively. I want to tell you that the gift as a compliment is one of the numerous tactics we adopted to get what we wanted timely. To make gift is not being foolish or wasteful. It means alot in government circle, expecially in Africa. So I will appreciate if you can still come up with something especially at this stage. If all are so expensive that you cannot purchase, please leave the wrist watches for us while you buy the rest.

Please reach me as early as possibly.

Best Regards.

Dr. Emma Johnson

This communication revealed that the good doctor was not a she, but a he. I wondered how many times in my recent correspondences I had referred to him as a her. Oh well, it must be a common mistake.

Then I noticed that the doc's timing was off a few days, as I believed I had already received the documents mentioned. I had to agreed that he and his wife must have worked hard to pull this together.

The last paragraph revealed that, once again, it was *my* fault things have been slow in processing due to *my* lack of positive response to the doctor's request for some gifts. I never received such a list. I could only suppose that the wrist watches referred to would have been Rolexes.

I drafted a letter and faxed it. I considered that my to-the-point manner was appropriate. The good doctor and his associates needed to realize with whom they were in negotiations: an American businessman. "Gifts. Harumph!"

Dr. Johnson,
First thing is, I would like to apologize for my inability to communicate as often as you would like me to. I have had a hard month. I was in a wicked vehicle accident, then I lost my woman over the holidays, and then caught a bad cold, which turned to pneumonia. When it rains, it pours.

Second, I would like to thank you and your wife for you New Years best wishes, and send my to you in return.

Third, I have received most of your faxes, although I must have missed the one in which you outline the gifts you recommend I send to encourage a speedy transaction on the part of your government's officials. That doesn't matter much, anyhow, as I don't, we in America, don't believe in bribes, up front fees, or the like to encourage people to do their jobs. Nothing personal, it just goes against our way of doing business. We work on the idea of gratuities to reward a job well done.

As an alternative to the idea of "gifts" I will fax to you a letter to whomever it may concern stating that I will send all who assist us in this transaction a cash gratuity upon our collective success.

Awaiting the money,
Brian Wizard

I added a cover-all note, *"To whom it may concern,"* for those on the good doctor's end who might need to hear my mode of operation regarding rewards for a job well done.

To whom it may concern,

In recognition of your jobs well done in regards to assisting Dr. Johnson and his team in all transactions a cash gratuity will be sent to you upon completion of said transactions.

In advance, I thank you for your speedy attention and diligent work. Your efforts will be generously rewarded.

Yours truly,
Brian Wizard

* * *

I realized that the time to act was fast approaching. After all these months the only thing that had transpired was a constant banter of promises. Why? It was no doubt *my* fault. It was *m e* who had failed to pay-the-money.

Admittedly, I wanted to move this investigation into the hands-on stage. For me that is always the best part of an investigation, and where the true story exists. All the promises and arrangements had become nothing more than senseless chatter. I hate senseless chatter, although I too can put forth hours of it at a time. Don't get me started.

I could see myself jumping feet-first from the frying pan into the fire. That's not a bad thing. I'm quite comfortable in the frying pan. I compare the fire to a walk on the beach. It's all a matter of perspective.

When to jump, that was the question. I wouldn't need much more than an invitation. Maybe Abba's contact in Spain, Mr. Philips, would provide the invitation?

Two faxes arrived in mid-January. The first fax was from Dr. Emma:

DR. EMMA JOHNSON BSC., ICAN., MBA.,Ph.D.
EXECUTIVE CHAIRMAN
CONTRACT AWARD COMMITTEE (N.N.P.C)
IKOYI – LAGOS NIGERIA
TEL/FAX: 234-90-405410

January 13, 2000

Dear Mr. Brian Wizard,

I received your fax dated Jan. 7, 2000.

I am sorry because I feel for you for all that you are passing through. I pray that God sees you through.

There is no point to talk about the gifts anymore because we could not have allowed that or any other thing else to delay or stall the deal for us. We know the way businesses are conducted here, especially within the Government establishments just as you know Americans' well too. America and Nigeria are of two different stocks of people, cultures, values and understanding. Forget about the gift for we have solved that.

To the best of my knowledge and capability, we have done essentially everything necessary to get the fund paid to you, hence are only waiting for confirmation of the fund from your side.

Besides Central bank of Nigeria which is slowing down the process, the fund should have, entered your account by now.

So let us keep in touch.

Regards,

DR. EMMA JOHNSON

Emma bought my story about all of my contrived woes, and prayed for me. How thoughtful.

More thoughtfulness was revealed in the statement that the good doctor had done everything to get the funds *". . . paid to you,"* and they were waiting confirmation from me that the funds had already been transferred into my account. I liked the part where it said *". . . necessary to get the funds paid to you"* and *". . . the funds should have, entered your account by now."*

"Damn! Wouldn't that just blow me away," I squealed.

I called my bank. "Hi, it's Brian Wizard. Would you check my account and tell me if any money has been deposited lately? I'm expecting a large sum from Africa."

"Not with a balance of forty-three dollars," the teller reported. "Sorry."

"Not nearly as sorry as I," I retorted.

The second fax was from the Central Bank of Nigeria. It provided a new family member's name and phone number. This one in Amsterdam. I made the call, but there was no answer.

CENTRAL BANK OF NIGERIA

DEPARTMENT OF DEBT MANAGEMENT
TINUBU SQUARE, LAGOS
DIRECT FAX LINE: 234-1-7595652

TO: MR. BRIAN WIZARD
P.O.BOX 42, WALLOWA
OR 97885, USA.

ATTN: MR. BRIAN WIZARD

DEAR SIR,

Date: JANUARY 12, 2000

Ref: CBN/FGN:021-VOL.5

STRICTLY CONFIDENTIAL

YOUR CONTRACT PAYMENT: THIRTY TWO MILLION U.S. DOLLARS, VIDE CONTRACT NO: NNPC/PED/2021-D:97

CENTRAL BANK OF NIGERIA (CBN) WISHES TO CONFIRM RECEIPT OF **NNPC PAYMENT ORDER** AND SUBSEQUENT **EXCHANGE CONTROL APPROVAL** FROM THE MINISTER OF FINANCE IN YOUR FAVOUR AND IN RESPECT OF THE ABOVE REFERENCED CONTRACT.

UNFORTUNATELY, DUE TO THE DELAY BY THE NATIONAL ASSEMBLY (SENATE AND THE LOWER HOUSE) TO PASS THE APPROPRIATION AND YEAR 2000 BUDGET BILL, THERE IS PAUCITY OF FUND.

THIS DEVELOPMENT HAS MADE IT IMPOSSIBLE FOR US TO EFFECT TRANSFER OF YOUR FUND ENROUTE LONDON, PROMPTLY.

HOWEVER, THE URGENCY WITH WHICH WE ARE DIRECTED TO DISPOSE OF THIS PAYMENT HAS OBLIGED US TO USE **NNPC OFFSHORE PAYMENT TRUSTEES** IN AMSTERDAM - NETHERLAND (**CASHFLOW INTERNATIONAL**). INCIDENTALLY YOUR NAME HAS BEEN INCLUDED IN THE AMSTERDAM LIST AND CBN IS PLEASED TO INFORM YOU THAT YOU CAN NOW RECEIVED YOUR PAYMENT THROUGH CASHFLOW INTERNATIONAL WITHOUT ANY FURTHER DELAY.

87

ALREADY YOUR FILE HAS BEEN HANDED OVER TO THEM WITH INSTRUCTION TO PAY YOU PROMPTLY THROUGH THEIR DIRECT **CASH VOTE ALLOCATION AND DISBURSEMENT (CVAD) FACILITY** IN AFFILIATION WITH CHEMICAL BANK.

FOR FINAL LIQUADATION OF THIS DEBT, YOU WOULD BE REQUIRED TO GO TO AMSTERDAM TO SIGN OFF THE PAYMENT IN ORDER TO RECEIVED YOUR CREDIT ACCORDINGLY.

THEREFORE, YOU ARE ADVISED TO CONTACT **DR. HERRY SAMUEL** AT CASHFLOW INTERNATIONAL ON TELEPHONE NUMBER **0031-625-556485 EXT. 207** TO CONFIRM DATE OF YOUR ARRIVAL.

THE PROCEDURE AND FURTHER INSTRUCTION, IF ANY, SHALL BE GIVEN TO YOU BY THE OFFICIALS OF CASHFLOW.

PLEASE KEEP US UPDATED FOR OUR ACCOUNTS AND RECORD PURPOSES.

CONGRATULATION SIR.

REGARDS,

DR. MOHAMMED M. SANI
DEPUTY - GOVERNOR. CBN.

I had to fax this note to Emma:

Brian Wizard
USA,

Dr. Johnson,
I have received your latest fax of 1/13/2000. In it you state that the 32 million should be in my account by now. No deposit has been made into my account, as of yet.
I did receive a fax from the Central Bank of Nigeria stating that I need to personally go to Amsterdam to sign off on the contract. Now, is this true? Please advise me on how I should interpret the two different scenarios.

I await your instructions,
Brian Wizard

* * *

On my next visit to the office, Mo's contact in Benin, Koffie at Trans-World Security Company, contacted me with this fax:

TRANS - WORLD SECURITY

COMPANY

COTONOU - REPUBLIC OF BENIN
AVENUE JEAN PAUL II
03 BP : 25347 Recette Principale
TEL/FAX : 229 – 30 – 59 - 11

Cotonou, 14ᵀᴴ JANUARY 2000

ATTN: MR. BRAIN WIZARD
         FAX : 1 – 541- 8860119
         U. S. A.

Dear MR. BRAIN WIZARD,

Fraternal greeting to you and HAPPY NEW YEAR.

It has been a long time we last heard from you regarding your Consignment Funds **(U.S.$25MILLION)** still pending in our Security Vault uncollected.

This is to inform you that it is very important you contact this Office immediately on this subject and confirm to this Office your present position on this issue. Now that you cannot send funds to enable us assist you to conclude the payment.

You are now required to come down to Cotonou personally for the purpose of signing all original Documents and opening of the Special Dollar Domiciliary Account in the presence of the Bank Officials and Transworld Security Officials.

Please contact this office only on TEL/FAX N°229 –30- 59-11.

Thanks for your cooperation.

My Warmest Regards.

Director Delivery & Operations.

"Too bad, Koffie. I'm not coming to yellow fever-infested Benin. Not even for twenty-five million dollars. Not when I have other options."

I remembered a news article I had read on one of the Nigerian newspapers' website. It reported a story about the mayor of a Benin town who was *"suspected"* of being part of a bank robbery. His countrymen's idea of a fair trial was to take the man from his house, douse him with gasoline and set him ablaze. If they thought I was guilty of stealing millions of their neighbor's looted funds, I could see how I would not escape a summary trial and torturous execution.

Spain, yes. Benin, no.

* * *

Abba had this e-mail waiting from me when I arrived at my office late one day. I was running late due to my need to move snow for six hours.

Mohammed K Abacha,1/14/00 4:56 AM -0700,STILL WAITING.   1

```
X-From_: mabacha@eudoramail.com  Fri Jan 14 03:56:51 2000
To: bwizard@eoni.com
Date: Fri, 14 Jan 2000 03:56:09 -0800
From: "Mohammed K Abacha" <mabacha@eudoramail.com>
Mime-Version: 1.0
X-Sent-Mail: off
Subject: STILL WAITING.
X-Sender-Ip: 194.204.253.198
Organization: QUALCOMM Eudora Web-Mail  (http://www.eudoramail.com:80)

ATTN:-Mr.BRIAN WIZARD.

I AM STILL WAITING YOUR ANSWER , ARE YOU NOW IN SPAIN ? ,IF NOT PLEASE ARRANGE YOUR TRIP TO SPAIN TO
MEET MR.ROGERS HE WILL BE THERE AT HIS OFFICE 15-01-2000 AND I HOPE TO CALL MR.ROGERS PHILIPS
IMMIDIATLY TO ARRANGE WITH HIM AND PICK UP THE BOXES IN  THEIR VAULT AT SECURITY COMPANY IN SPAIN.

I AM WAITING YOUR RESPECTABLE ANSWER AND KEEP IN TOUCH WITH ME FOR ANY DEVELOPPEMMT .

MR.ABBA ABACHA.
```

I immediately drafted this note, then faxed it to Mr. Philips.

Brian Wizard
P.O.Box 42
Wallowa, Or. 97885   1/17/00
541 886 0119
Mr. Philips,

I have been trying to contact you on behalf of Mr. Abacha of West Africa. It is my belief that you have two, or more galvanized boxes with my name on them for me to sign off on. Our time difference is so great that I keep missing your presence at your office, so I have decided faxes would be a better form of communication.

I have business in Holland, Germany, Belieze and South Africa as well as with you. I am trying to organize an all in one travel itinerary that will be to my benefit. What I need to know is when you will be in your office, or who I can carry out this transaction with if you are not available, as you are not this week. I need to know exactly what you will require from me in regards to time and other matters. Please inform me of these things so I can arrange my travel around that time schedule.

Do you have an e-mail address? If so, please write to me at: bwizard@eoni.com. This form of communication is the best form for me once I begin my travels.

I await you response via fax at the above number, or e-mail, if you have it. Or, you can leave a voice message on the same above number.

I await your instructions.

Brian Wizard

I sent this e-mail to Abba:

Abba,

I continue to call and fax Mr. Philips in Spain, but to no avail. I can't tell you what is happening there, or anything. I will not travel to Spain until I receive a confirmation from Mr. Philips that he will be there to meet me. I am sure you understand that.

Brian Wizard

My internal combat-ready lamp light was green: safe and comfy. That is not to say that the mercury was not rising. I could feel the pressure building. Action had to begin soon.

Dr. Emma sent this fax:

From: Dr. Emma Johnson   *January 17, 2000*
          Lagos – Nigeria.

To: Mr. Brian Wizard

Dear Sir,

I have received your fax, latest.

Having completed everything at this end, we are dubious, hence presumed that the Fund is there. If the Fund is not yet and you have received a letter to that effect from CBN it means the money is on its way.

Regarding the CBN instruction, I have checked that this morning and found out it is true.

You are required to go to Amsterdam personally. So please reach the officer in Amsterdam as soon as possible and do your best to fly without waste of time.

Regards,

Dr. Emma Johnson

The first paragraph sounded great! If they were to send the money, I'd go nowhere. I'd stop my investigation and become a money manager. A career change could be good for me.

See, that's just how easy it was to believe that the scam was the truth. The second paragraph dispelled my brief moment of delusion.

The third paragraph pushed the pressure gauge up a notch, just shy of switching the combat-ready lamp to yellow: Get ready and stay ready.

I could most definitely go to Amsterdam! Legal gambling. Legal prostitution. Legal hash and weed! Not having been to the great city of Amsterdam since the early seventies, I felt assured that a secondary investigation regarding the liberal society of the Netherlands could make my primary investigation of the scam a win-win situation. I would not come home empty handed. A story resides within the coffee shop industry of Amsterdam, I was sure.

"Good on you, Emma!" I shouted.

*   *   *

I could fly to Amsterdam and see Dr. Samuel, then drive to Spain and meet with Mr. Philips. I was having a hard time making contact with both parties. Until I had confirmation that they would be available to meet with me within a short time frame, I would not go. I had to make it clear that I would not be able to wait around for anyone. I told Dr. Emma that much in this fax:

Dr. Johnson,

I have called Mr. Samuel twice, and both times he has not been in. This time they said he will be gone all week. I left my number and they will call back. Of course, this all puts me in a situation. For me to actually go to Amsterdam it will take some logistical planning. I am also supposed to have business in Belieze, Spain, and South Africa, as well as Budapest. It would be wise on my part to organize a one time trip. This alone will take some timing to arrange flights. Not knowing exactly how long I will be needed in Spain and Amsterdam sort of makes it hard to plan. So, I wait to speak with Mr. Samuel to have him explain to me exactly what will be required of me and the time it will take. I will be doing the same with the business contact in Spain.

I have come to the conclusion that it will be best for me to simply leave my isolated estate in the wilderness for ten weeks in order to take care of all of this international business. I might as well take advantage of the harsh winter weather and let it be my estate's protector. It will take me a week to close it down and secure refuge for my livestock at another location. Once I am out of my estate, then I will begin my journey. I will work out of my office for a few days if I can, but I must take advantage of clear weather when it comes in order to make safe passage over the four major mountain passes I must cross to get anywhere near an airport. I will most likely head for the San Francisco Bay area in California since I have friends and relative to stay with whilst I organize my travel. This will take some time. Of course, my first conversation with Mr. Samuel in Amsterdam over the phone will be an attempt to bypass the need of my actual presence. In this day and age of electronics I don't know why I personally need to go. We'll see.

On a personal matter, I hate air travel as I tend to get sick from the recycled air. But for you, and our arrangement I will risk my health, my life. I hope you appreciate that. I'm sure you do.

93

I see that we both must exercise patience. I will check with the bank first thing tomorrow, just in case the money went through. That would be so much better.

Now, what are your plans after I have received the money? Are you coming to the States, or should we meet elsewhere? Will we meet at all? Please explain to me soon, before I go on this long journey, what the next part of the plan is. The follow through should be laid out now. Once I am away from my office, communication will be difficult. You do not have e-mail? If you can, get an e-mail account set up. I would make communication so much faster and easier, as well as accessible.

The decision to act was going to come as quickly as the bite of an Australian "no see 'em" sandfly. I felt the pressure to act build inside me as I entered my office on a cold and snowy January afternoon. I didn't have much time to stay downtown, as I still had to bring in firewood, do the dishes and clean my house before the early winter night made all these tasks that much harder to perform.

Abba wrote me this:

Mohammed K Abacha,1/18/00 5:01 AM -0700,Update.

```
X-From_: mabacha@eudoramail.com  Tue Jan 18 04:02:13 2000
To: bwizard@eoni.com
Date: Tue, 18 Jan 2000 04:01:35 -0800
From: "Mohammed K Abacha" <mabacha@eudoramail.com>
Mime-Version: 1.0
Cc: bwizard@eoni.com
X-Sent-Mail: off
X-Expiredinmiddle: true
Subject: Update.
X-Sender-Ip: 194.204.253.203
Organization: QUALCOMM Eudora Web-Mail  (http://www.eudoramail.com:80)

ATTN :-BRIAN WIZARD.


I HAVE RECEIVED YOUR E-MAIL .CONTENTS CAREFULLY UNDERSTOOD.

MR. ROGER PHILIP WAS NOT IN THE OFFICE HIS TELEPHONE / FAX IN SPAIN IS +35 91 610 6046 OR +34 64 904
0330. HE IS NOW IN SWITZERLAND YOU SHOULD TRY AGAIN TO CONTACT HIM , I FURNISH TO YOU HIS WORLDNET OR
GLOBAL TELEPHONE NO :
( Satilit n0 )-881 625 620 934 WITHOUT CODE EARE ,PLEASE YOU CONTACT HIM IMMEDIATELY TO ENABLE URGENT
FINALISATION  OF YOU PICKING UP THE FUNDS FROM THEIR VAULT.TO AVOID FURTHER DELAY  KINDLY CONTACT HIM
AS SOON AS POSSIBLE.

I AM GLAD THAT YOU HAVE ALL THE PROOFS AS REGARDS PICKING UP THE  FUNDS FROM THEIR VAULT.HOWEVER I
QUITE APPRECIATE YOU BEING HIGHLY LEARNED AND WELL TO DO.

MAY THE ALMIGHTY ALLAH BLESS YOU AND YOUR FAMILY.AWAITING YOUR PROMPT REPLY ASAP.

BEST REGARDS,

MR. ABBA ABACHA.
```

With Philips in Switzerland, why would I be heading to Spain? I wondered what paperwork Abba was talking about. My Benin paper-work? I thought it was time to put us on the same page with this e-mail reply:

Mohammed K Abacha, 1/18/00 1:32 AM -0700, Re: Update.　　　　　　　**1**

```
     To: "Mohammed K Abacha" <mabacha@eudoramail.com>
   From: Brian Wizard <bwizard@eoni.com>
Subject: Re: Update.
     Cc:
    Bcc:
X-Attachments:

Abba Abacha,
        I was told to wait until Friday to contact Spain. What I doubt is that I have the proper
paperwork for the money in Spain. The paperwork I have is for money in another country, a different
security company. What I will no doubt need is a Clearance Certificate from the Nigerian National Drug
Law Agency stating that the money is free and clear of money laundering and drug affiliation, with my
name on it. Plus, a certificate of ownership of the money in the vaults in Spain, with my name on it.
Plus any diplomatic channel paperwork that will also state that I, Brian Wizard, is the owner of the
boxes, the money, etc.
        Who will have those papers? You? Or Mr. Roger Philips? I will need all of this paperwork
before I depart. This will cause delay if I have to wait too long for them. See what you can do about
all of this. I'm sure you want this transaction to be swift and convenient for us all. I await the
results of your labor and inquires.
                                        Yours truly,
                                        Brian Wizard
```

My life had become rather hectic. I hadn't finished my new outbuilding due to the snowfall. Plowing and snowblowing used up all my spare time. I had been shoveling out from ten to fourteen inches of snowfall each night. My butt was starting to drag from all the extreme manual labor that comes with keeping my roads and paths open. Add the daily trips to town for monitoring the various scam activists to the other mundane aspects of life and I was reaching critical burnout stage. Leaving behind all the work that comes with winter in the wilderness would truly alleviate most of my hardships. This was like being in the military and waiting for combat orders. You know they are coming, but they haven't arrived yet.

Packing up to leave my estate would itself take a few days. I had to consider the weather when it came to my departure. I had four mountain passes to negotiate no matter what direction I went. The nearest airport I would fly out of was two hundred and fifty miles away. The furthest was nine hundred miles away.

Abba came through with this e-mail next:

Mohammed K Abacha,1/19/00 12:45 PM -0700,Please Try.

```
X-From_: mabacha@eudoramail.com  Wed Jan 19 11:45:49 2000
To: bwizard@eoni.com
Date: Wed, 19 Jan 2000 11:45:01 -0800
From: "Mohammed K Abacha" <mabacha@eudoramail.com>
Mime-Version: 1.0
X-Sent-Mail: off
Subject: Please Try.
X-Sender-Ip: 194.204.253.198
Organization: QUALCOMM Eudora Web-Mail  (http://www.eudoramail.com:80)
```

ATTN:-Mr.BRIAN WIZARD.

YOU SHOULD KEEP TRYING TO ESTABLISH CONTACT WITH Mr.ROGERS PHILIPS JUST BE PATIENCE AND CONTINUE TO DIAL UNTIL YOU ARE FINALLY THROUGH.

KEEP ME POSTED AND GET BACK TO ME WITH BRIEFS OF THE PROGRESS IN ARRANGING TO PICK UP THE FUNDS FROM THEIR VAULT ,THIS FUNDS WILL BE INVESTED IN ANY PROFIT ORIENTED PROJECT IN YOUR COUNTRY AND AS SOON AS THE CASE OF MY ELDER BROTHER IS OVER BY THE GRACE OF ALLAH(GOD) AND IMMEDIATELY OUR TRAVEL DOCUMENTS IS RELEASED TO US ,I PERSONNALLY WILL VISIT YOU IN YOUR LOCATION FOR MUTUAL UNDERSTANDING AND BENEFITS.

YOU WILL BE STAY IN SPAIN ONLY ONE WEEKS , MAY ALLAH PROTECT AND GUIDE US AWAITING YOUR EARLIEST REPLY.

BEST REGARDS .

Mr.ABBA ABACHA.

I kept calling Philips, but to no avail.

I wondered if Abba really meant it when he said he'd come visit me personally.

*   *   *

The weather took a break from its nightly dumping of the beautiful white stuff. I headed to town early, just in case the weather changed. I was feeling physically tired. Moving tons of snow is a full-body workout. At the same time, I was feeling rather buff. Buff is exactly how I wanted to be when I met with any members of my African scam family.

Abba, who continued to be the most active player of the four separate scam factions, sent me this e-mail:

X-From_: mohammed.abacha@eudoramail.com Fri Jan 21 09:07:32 2000
To: bwizard@eoni.com
Date: Fri, 21 Jan 2000 09:06:45 -0800
From: "Mohammed K Abacha" <mohammed.abacha@eudoramail.com>
Mime-Version: 1.0
Cc: bwizard@eoni.com
X-Sent-Mail: off
Subject: Top Urgent.
X-Sender-Ip: 194.204.253.207
Organization: QUALCOMM Eudora Web-Mail (http://www.eudoramail.com:80)

ATTN: -MR.BRIAN WIZARD.

I HAVE RECEIVED YOUR E-MAIL OF 20TH JAN 2000, WITH GREAT JOY ,CONTENTS CAREFULLY .

SIR , FOR YOUR INFORMATION , MY MOTHER WAS CALLED ON THE FEDERAL GOVERNMENT (HEAD OF STATE OF
NIGERIA), TO COME TO OUR AND START "AS SOON AS POSSIBLE " TO TAKE CARE OF OUR FAMILY AS DONE TO
FAMILIES OF LATE OR RETIRED HEADS OF STATE , BECAUSE WE HAVE ONLY BEEN SURVIVING ON THE GOODWIL OF
FRIENDS IN KANO ,AFTER THE NIGERIAN AUTHORITIES WAS PERMITTED ME WITH MY MOTHER Mrs.MARYAM ABACHA TO
VISIT MY ELDER BROTHER MOHAMMED ABACHA AND I HAVE DISCUSSED WITH HIM IN DETAILS HE TOLD ME TO SHOW YOU
SOMETHlNGS ABOUT OUR BUSINESS.

THIS DATA GIVEN TO YOU ABOUT THE FUNDS HAS BEEN REGISTERED IN YOUR NAME   (MR.BRIAN WIZARD) , AND
SENT OUT OF NIGERIA THROUGH THE DIPLOMATIC CHANNEL AND WITH THE HELP OF HIGHER OFFICERS FOR FORMER
DIRECTOR OF MILITARY INTELLIGENCE AND FORMER COMMISSIONER OF POLICE AND ALSO NATIONAL INTELLIGENCE
AGENCY , THE FUNDS SENT TO SEVERAL FOREIGN ACCOUNTS ABROAD FOR SAFER KEEPER OR SECURITY COMPANIES
.VAULT , FOR YOU TO RECEIVE IT AS THE OWNER THIS FUNDS ORIGINAL FOR OUR FATHER FORMER NIGERIAN HEAD OF
STATE ,GENERAL SANI ABACHA WHO DIED ON 8TH DAY OF JUNE 1998 WHILE STILL ON ACTIVE DUTY TO OUR NATION ,
BUT WE WAS AFRAID TO RECOVER OR FREEZE IT BY NEW CIVILIAN GOVENMENT , ANYWAY THE TOTAL OF THE FUNDS IS
10 BILLIONS UNITED STATE DOLLARS , 15 % OF THE TOTAL SUM WILL BE YOUR SHARE OR COMMISSION WHILE THE
REMAINING 85 % WILL BE FOR MYSELF AND MY FAMILY WHICH WE WILL USE FOR INVESTMENTS PURPUESE IN YOUR
COUNTRY THROUGH YOUR HELP.

THIS IS A LIST INCLUDINGS NAMES OF COUNTRIES AS FOLLOW:
-SPAIN : 2 BILLIONS $ IN SECURITY COMPANY VAULT.
-SWISSD: 2 BILLIONS $IN BANKS FOR SAFEKEEPER .
-DENMARK:81 MILLIONS $ IN SECURITY COMPANY VAULT.
-GERMANY : 260 MILLIONS $ IN SECURITY COMPANY VAULT.
-NETHERLAND : 650 MILLIONS $ IN SECURITY COMPANY VAULT.
-GANA: 9 MILLIONS $ IN BANKS FOR SAFEKEEPER .
-ENGLAND:3 BILLIONS $ IN BANKS FOR SAFEKEEPER .
-UNITED STATE:795 MILLIONS $ IN BANKS FOR SAFEKEEPER.
-SOUTH AFRICA:70 MILLIONS $ IN BANKS FOR SAFEKEEPER.
-CANADA:200 MILLIONS $IN BANKS FOR SAFEKEEPER .
-IVORY COAST:40 MILLIONS $ IN SECURITY COMPANY VAULT.
-SOUTH KORIA : 1 BILLIONS $ IN SECURITY COMPANY VAULT.
-AUSTRALIA: 2 BILLIONS $ IN BANKS FOR SAFE KEEPER .
MOREOVER , ANOTHER 10 BILLIONS HAS BEEN REGISTERED IN OTHER PERSON'S NAME FROM ARABIC COUNTRY, I WILL
SEND YOU HIS DETAILS SOON TO INTRODUCE WITH HIM , IT IS ONLY MYSELF AND MY ELDER BROTHER THAT KNOWS
ABOUT THIS FUNDS LOGDED IN THE VAULT OF THE SECURITY COMPANIES OR FOREIGN ACCOUNTS FOR SAFEKEEPER ,
MOREOVER IT IS IMPOSSIBLE TO SAVE THE FILES OR DOCUMENTS FOR A LOT FO FUNDS IN MY HOME OR IN NIGERIA ,
MY BROTHER WAS SAVED IT IN TOP SECURE PLACE AND THE COPIES WITH DIRECTORS OF THE FINANCIAL COMPANIES.

THE DATA 'S OF THE PERSONS IN ENGLAND , SPAIN AND CANADA WILL BE ASSIST YOU AS FOLLOWS:
-MR.ROGERS PHILIPS THE MANAGING DIRECTOR OF SECURITY COMPANY IN SPAIN HIS TELEPHONE NUMERS : +34
91610 6046 * +34 64904 0330 *HIS WORLD NET MOBLE PHONE :+881 625 620 934 .
-MR.ANTHONY SMITH THE MANAGING DIRECTOR OF CITIBANK OF CANADA ,HIS TELEPHONE NUMBERS :+1 416 829 9027
*FAX :+1 416 633 9808 * HIS BANK OFFICE NO:+1 416 299 2688.
-MR.A.IBRAHIM DANGOTE THE MANAGING DIRECTOR OF SECURITY COMPANY HIS TELEPHONE NUMBERS :+44 186 539
5117 * +44 70 50 60 95 07 *+44 70 50 66 06 36 *+44 79 30 20 23 41 HIS MOBLE FAX: +870 761900 837. TELL
THEM THAT YOU ARE FOREIGN PARTNER OF MOHAMMED ABACHA AND HIS FAMILY.

IN FACT , I DON' T REALLY KNOW EXACTLY IF YOU HAVE PAPER WORK FOR THE MONEY FALLACY OR NOT !!!, FOR
THE REASON I WAS ASKED YOU TO E-MAIL ATTACHMENT YOUR CERTIFICATES . MY BROTHER THINK THAT HE WILL BE

STAY A LONG IN HIGH COURT WITH FATHER'S CHIEF SECURITY OFFICERS BECAUSE THEY ACCUSED MURDER OF KUDIRAT
ABIOLA WIFE OF LATE OPPOSITION POLITICIAN MOSHOOD ABIOLA SO , HE HAS GIEVN ME THE FULL AUTHORITY   TO
TAKE ANY DECISION CONECRNING OUR TRANSACTION , YOU HAD BETTER NOW TO DECIDE WHETHER TO TRAVEL TO
SPAIN AND TO ASSIST MY FAMILY OR NOT ...???, IF YES YOU SHOULD KEEP UPDATE ME AS SOON AS YOU GET IN
TOUCE THE ABOVE MANAGER DIRECTORS , BUT IF YOUR ANSWER ..NOT I WILL BE IMMEDIATELY SEEK FOR ANOTHER
ASSISTANCE IF YOU DO NOT SOUND POSITIVE , NOW THE BALL IS TRULY IN YOUR COURT AND YOU SHOULD KICK THE
BALL IN MY DIRECTION .

BEST REGARDS.

97

MR.ABBA ABACHA.

I scanned through all the redundant Abacha family woes, but slowed my reading to word-by-word when I came across the new numbers. My heart accelerated. My tongue started flapping as I said, "TWENTY-TWO BA-BA-BILLION!" This second Mohammed knew how to get my attention.

I read my cut. "What?" I complained. "A meager fifteen percent! What's with the decrease, Mo?" I did some math and my disappointment diminished with the deduction that three billion mega-bucks and change would be my share.

I slowly perused the list of countries and the amounts of money waiting for me to pick up. Yep, so much for winter. "Good-bye frozen fog, beautiful snow, and cold winds a-blowin.'"

Where to go first? I glanced through the rest of the e-mail. I was in a mild state of shock. Too many possibilities.

"Yo," Martin called out, soon to enter my office. "What's up?"

"It happened, man. They did it." I eluded the details of what I meant, just to set the stage for delivery.

"Who? The Africans? They sent the money!" Martin's excitement swelled.

"No. No money sent. The numbers went up a bit, though. Not to one, nor two, not three or four. How about a whopping twenty-two billion. BILLION WITH A CAPITAL B!" I shouted, "And change."

I printed Abba's recent e-mail and handed it to my friend.

"Damn!" Martin said in his mimicable fashion.

I joined him, and we said together, "Wish this weren't a scam."

"So, what are you going to do? Does this turn the combat-ready lamp to yellow?" Martin asked.

"Not yet. I need to do little more work on this. It will be a hands-on investigation soon enough, though. Soon enough."

While Martin read the entire e-mail, I read the last part again. Three contacts' names with numbers. Spain. England, and Canada. I could see the greatest advantage in going to Canada. It's so close.

The last paragraph I also found very interesting. Abba didn't know if I had correct paperwork, either. He made it clear that he had the authority to act on completing these transactions.

"Oh, look!" I said happily to Martin, bringing him to the last part of the paragraph. "Abba is a soccer player. I love the metaphor. Stand prepared to received the ball, buddy."

With Martin watching, I drafted and sent this e-mail:

Mohammed K Abacha,1/21/00 1:18 AM -0700,Re: Top Urgent.   1

```
        To: "Mohammed K Abacha" <mohammed.abacha@eudoramail.com>
      From: Brian Wizard <bwizard@eoni.com>
   Subject: Re: Top Urgent.
        Cc:
       Bcc:
X-Attachments:
```

Mr. Abacha,

     Am I to understand that you want me to pick up all of this money? If so, not a problem. I will need paperwork for it all, that is probably the biggest problem, yet not a problem that cannot be overcome with your help. You say there is money here in the US. Why don't you let me get that first. It would be the easiest. I can drive there. Or the Bank in Cananda. I shall call there immediately to find out which city and what will be require of me.

     I am all for helping you out, especially if I have all the proper paperwork, etc. to make the process smooth, legal and convenient. I do not have a scanner for my computer. If you have a fax available I could fax documents to you. I will find a scanner if not. I'll buy one.

     Now, let it be understood that I have spent the last week securing my estate by dismantling all of its working operations. I have done this so that I can travel. I am awaiting the next serious snowstorm so that I can close down the road to my estate by creating huge snow barriers. After that, I will wait only for the next clear travel day and will begin my journey. It will take three days to drive to San Francisco, or two days to Seattle, where I will have access to airports.

     Now that I have thought it over, I will work the Canadian connection first. It makes the most sense.

     I would feel very much relieved if I could have some earnest money sent from you, directly or indirectly, to quell my doubts of the integrity of this business proposal. Why? You know as well as I do that the infamous Nigerian 419 scam works exactly like this business proposal. Especially when it comes to me paying up-front fees, etc. A meager contribution of $5000-$10,000 would enrich my soul with such interest and trust that I will work like a whirl wind in stirring up all of the business you have proposed. Think it over, let me know if you can do this, just to calm my curiosity and nerves. The Nigerian 419 Scam is big news over here. I don't know if you know that, or not. Send any money you can via Western Union to Brian Wizard, Enterprise, Or. Do this soon, before I depart the area, please.

     Personally, I have faith in your proposal. You stand to gain freedom from it. I can only hope that with my encouragement you will move beyond all of your current woes and build a new life, one of beauty and pleasantness for you, your family and all the people who come in contact with you.

     I also believe you are a devout Muslim and believe in the words of the Koran. Therefore, I have reason to trust you and this business proposal. So, my response is very positive. I have worked hard to abandon my estate, my pleasant life, in order to assist you.

     When talking with your brother, did he say that he is familiar with me, or not? He should be.

     My first goal will be to go to another country, one with liberal banking laws, to set up an account to transfer all of the funds. This sounds good, yes?

     With the Canadian money to be the first on my list to secure, the US money the second, all actions will then become swift and accurate. My fears will subside, my knowledge increased and my performance enhanced. I will need from you, directly or indirectly, moral support, instructions, hopefully the earnest money, and later a hearty handshake of success. Does all of that sound logical to you? Let me know.

     I am now going to initiate the call to Canada. I will e-mail to you the results.
                            On the case,
                            Brian Wizard

    I started the e-mail with details that filled Abba in on what I had done to get ready for the journey to Spain, or wherever he needed me to go. I felt confident that now would be a good time to add something new from my end. A request for some earnest money felt right.

    "If they send up-front money to help pay the expenses, I'll be shocked," I told Martin.

"Would it mean that this isn't a scam?" Martin asked, his hope rekindled. His butt rested on the very edge of the chair, as he leaned toward me. He held Abba's e-mail with both hands. His eyes asked for confirmation that the scam was the truth and there really was money coming this way. Lots of money.

"Damn!" was all I needed to say. Martin knew the rest of the sentence.

I then called Mr. Anthony Smith in Canada, but all I received was a fax tone. I drafted this note to him and faxed it:

Brian Wizard
P.O.Box 42
Wallowa, Or. 97885 USA
541 886 0119 (fax/tele)

1/21/00

Mr. Anthony Smith,

   I am the foreign partner of the Abacha family and I have been instructed to contact you regarding funds in your bank that are in my name and are to be dispersed to me. I will be contacting you on Monday at the phone number: 416 299 2688. If this number is not correct, please fax to me at the above number one that is correct.

   I would also like for you to tell my the exact location of your bank, which will make my journey so much easier.

   I look forward to meeting with you very soon.

Yours truly,
Brian Wizard

Then I thought, what if I combined one Abba contact, say the one in London, with Emma's Amsterdam contact? It could be advantageous for me to work two different scam factions in two different countries during the same trip. Were they both parts of the same international crime conspiracy, or were they independent from one another? Do they operate exactly the same, or were there variations to the game? Could I manipulate one to pay the expenses of the other? The answers to these questions would only come by being physically involved.

"If I go anywhere, one place will be Amsterdam," I emphatically stated to Martin. He could only raise his eyebrows at my potential for fun.

The biggest problem was my inability to contact Dr. Samuel. I drafted this note and faxed it to Dr. Emma:

Brian Wizard
P.O.Box 42
Wallowa, Or. 97885 USA
541 886 0119 (tele/fax)

1/22/00

Dr. Johnson,

I have not been able to contact Dr. Samuel. He appears to be out of the country. Is there a way, which there should be in this day and age of electronics, for me to have the necessary forms faxed to me at the above number, then I can have my signature notarized and duly recorded here, the post the papers with my original signature back to Amsterdam, so that the funds can be transferred at that time. This will speed things up and is completely the same as if I actually went to Amsterdam.

My presence is being requested in Hong Kong and Viet Nam. So, I am torn as to which direction to go. I hope my above suggestion will work this matter of ours to a fruitful closure.

What do you think about that?

Yours truly,
Brian Wizard.

Relief came in his next fax:

DR. EMMA JOHNSON BSC., ICAN., MBA.,Ph.D.

EXECUTIVE CHAIRMAN
CONTRACT AWARD COMMITTEE (NNPC)
IKOYI - LAGOS NIGERIA.
TEL/FAX: 234-90-405410

January 24, 2000

Dear Dr. Wizard,

I have received all your messages. I really appreciate your effort to close the deal. Please do not relent until success is achieved. All our hopes for survival is rested on timely completion of the project.

There is no other way, other than for you to go to Amsterdam personally. I checked on the possibility of otherwise but no way.

All your time invested in this pursuit, as you are quite aware, will duly be compensated, personally.

101

"Okay, Doc. I'm off to Amsterdam as soon as Dr. Samuel makes contact," I said directly to the fax paper.

To my great surprise, there was also a fax from none other than Koffie, of Trans-World Security in Benin.

TRANS - WORLD SECURITY

COMPANY

COTONOU - REPUBLIC OF BENIN
AVENUE JEAN PAUL II
03 BP : 25347 Recette Principale
TEL/FAX : 229 – 30 – 59 - 11

Cotonou, 21st JANUARY 2000

ATTN: **MR. BRAIN WIZARD**
         FAX : 1 – 541- 886 - 0119
         U. S. A.

Dear MR. BRAIN WIZARD,

Fraternal greeting to you Sir. We hereby acknowledge receipt of your Fax message dated 15/01/2000 and the content quite clear.

For your information, this Consignment Funds **U.S.$25M** now in our Security Vault for Cash payment to you the Beneficiary, was directed by the Pacific International Merchant Bank (NIG.) PLC for cash payment to you on personal presentation through the Banking channels Via Telegraphic Transfer. The purpose of your personal presentation is for opening the Special Dollar Domiciliary Account, obtain the TTCC from the Ministry of Finance and signing of all original documentations in the presence of the Bank Officials and TWSC Officials.

It was due to your illhealth that you where exempted by the Management of TWSC not to come personally for the payment. While you were required and informed to send funds Via Western Union Money Transfer to enable us assist you in Opening the special Dollar Domiciliary Account; obtain the TTCC, Bullion Van and Stamp Duty from the Ministry of Justice to Legalize the funds Transfer in compliance with the Monetary Laws of this country your Attorney David Olatunde should proceed to Cotonou and witness the operations on the spot on your behalf.

This was the only help we strongly prepared to render to you due to your present health condition but you never comply.

As a matter of facts and honesty, to resolve this matter immediately is for you to send the required funds Via Western Union Money

Transfer as previously informed. If you accept to send the Money Via Western union, confirm some to me, and I will send to you the names to collect the money Via Western Union.

Alternatively, if you cannot send the money Via Western Union, to enable us help you in your absence there is nothing we can do, than to await for you until March when you will arrive Cotonou to Conclude the Transaction personally.

You are now required to send via fax your confirmed Banking Details and photocopy of your International passport pages **1& 2** to enable us update your File.

Thanks for your kind understanding and cooperation as we are now awaiting your urgent .reply.

My personal Best Regards.

KOFFI M. ...
Director : D...ve...ations.

With the option of traveling the world to pick up twenty-two billion dollars, why would I even consider going to yellow fever-infested Benin for a meager twenty-five million, or even five hundred million?

*   *   *

The combat-ready lamp switched to pale yellow, the first of three levels of caution: pale, amber, and bright. A change in the intensity of a situation would influence the level of precaution. Preparations began. I worked the internet for a price quote on airline tickets. Priceline.com came up with $459 round trip. I called my discount travel agent. She was on top of her game and beat the best internet price by thirty dollars.

I could fly from Seattle to London for $422 return. This flight had stops along the way. I didn't like that. I wanted non-stop. This changed the airport of departure to San Francisco, the airport nine hundred miles away.

"I still need confirmations from the other end," I explained to my travel agent before I put any money down for the tickets. "As soon as I have everyone in place and waiting, I'll go."

Abba e-mailed this note:

ATTN : -MR.BRIAN WIZARD .

I HAVE RECEIVED YOUR E-MAIL OF 24TH JAN,2000.
ON REFERENCE TO MY LAST A LETTER , I HAVE TO CORRECT SOME A DETAILS TO YOU REGARDING THE FUNDS HAS
BEEN DEPOSITED IN YOUR NAME BY MY ELDER BROTHER MR.MOHAMMED ABACHA.

CORRECTION OF THE FUNDS AS FOLLOWS / TOTAL OF THE FUNDS DEPOSITED UNDER YOUR NAME IS MORE THAN 10
BILLION $, EXACTLY WE TRUST YOU WITH 12 BILLION $(TWELVE BILLION UNITED STATE DOLLARS),IN CANADA IS
NOT 200 MILLIONS $ BUT ONLY 90 MILLIONS $ AND IN IVORY COAST IS NOT 40 MILLIONS $ BUT IS 45 MILLIONS $
, AND AS YOU KNOW SPAIN 2 BILLION $,SWITZERLAND 2 BILLIONS $,DENMARK 81 MILLIONS $, GERMANY 260
MILLIONS $,NETHERLAND 650 MILLIONS $, GANA 9 MILLIONS $,ENGLAND 3 BILLIONS $,UNITED STATE 795 MILLIONS
$,SOUTH AFRICA 70 MILLIONS $,SOUTH KORIA 1 BILLIONS $,AUSTRALIA 2 BILLIONS $.

SO , CALL THE SECURITY COMPANIES MANAGERS IN SPAIN AND ENGLAND IMMEDIATELY AND TELL THEM THAT YOU ARE
FOREIGN PARTNER TO ABACHA'S FAMILY THEY WILL TELL YOU ON WHAT TO DO THEN YOU CALL AND TELL ME WHAT YOU
FINALISE WITH THEM ,PLEASE DON'T WAITS TIME IN TO THIS TRANSACTIONS NOTE THAT YOU WOULD BE REQUERED TO
VISIT SPAIN AND ENGLAND TO SIGN AND RECEIVE THE BOXES , THE DIRECTORS OF SECURITY COMPANIES WILL
ARRANGE THE DELIVERY AND HAND YOU OVER THE CASH BOXES AND IT IS IMPOSSIBLE TO HANDOVER THE BOXES TO
ANYBODY , YOUR PRESENCE IS REQUIRED AT THE BANKS PREMISES SO YOU SHOULD CONTACT THE DIRECTORS OF
SECURITY COMPANIES TO ARRANGE WITH THEM .

9474100

Dr.ANTHONY SMITH ,CITIBANK'S SCARBOROUGH VILLAGE BRANCH ,UNIT # 33-3300 MIDLAND AVENUE TORONTO ,
ONTARIO M1V 4A1 ,CANADA .ITS TELEPHONE #:+1 416 299-2688,TELEPHONE HOME # :+1 416
829-9027.--//Dr.IBRAHIM DANGOTE ,NO 1 TUDOR MEWS HAWTHORNE ROAD ,WILLESON GREEN ,NW10 LONDON ,ENGLAND
,HIS TELEPHONE # :+44 70 50 609507 OR +44 70 50 609506 OR +44 18 65 395117 ,THIS PERSONS WILL GIVE YOU
ALL DOCUMENTS YOU NEED ABOUT FUNDS .I HAVE BEEN TOLD YOU THAT MY FAX AND TELEPHONE NUMBERS IS UNDER
STRICT SECURITY CHECKS AND YOU MUST NOT CALL ME OR FAX ME BECAUSE YOU WILL BE IN DANGER AND MOREOVER .
THE UNIT FORECE ARE EVERY DAY HEARING OUR CONVERSATIONS OR CALL VIA PHONE OR FAX OR AT HOME , THE BEST
AND EASY WAY IS TO SCAN YOUR DOCUMENTS AND TO SENT IT VIA E-MAIL ATTACHMENT AND TO STAY IN CONTACT
WITH ME BY INTERNT .

I KNOW THAT THERE IS IMFAMOUS NIGERIAN SCAM AND THEY ARE IMPERSONATED OUR FAMILY'S NAME YOU SHOULD NOT
AT ALL OPEN UP COMMUNICATION WITH THEM BECAUSE THEY ARE ALL HACKERS AND BUNDLE OF BULLSHIT AS REGARDS
THE FUNDS WHICH IS ALREADY STASHED OR DEPOSITED IN THE VAULT OF THE SECURITY COMPANIES IN ABOVE
COUNTRIES .

AS YOU KNOW THAT MY ELDER BROTHER MOHAMMED ABACHA WERE JAILED BY HEAD OF STATE Mr.OBASANJO ON 09TH
NOVEMBER 1999, HE HAS GEVEN THE INSTRUCTION TO HIS GOVENMENT TO FREEZE ALL OUR ACCOUNTS IN NIGERIA AND
OUT SIDE OF NIGERIA COINCIDED WITH SWITZERLAND,ENGALND,BRESIL,
UNITED STATE HAS ORDERED THE FREEZED OF ALL OUR BANK ACCOUNTS IN THE NAME OF GENERAL SANI ABACHA AND
HIS FAMILY Mrs.MARYAM ABACHA ,MOHAMMED ABACHA , ABBA ABACHA ,ZEINAB ABACHA , ABDULKADIR ABACHA (
FATHER'S BROTHER) AND HIS FAMILY TOO , THE FEDERAL OFFICE FOR POLICE AFFAIRE WITH THE CORRPORATION
F.B.I OF UNITED STATE OF AMERICA WAS FROZEN ALL OUR ACCOUNTS ALL AMERICAN BANK FOR EXEMPLE , BANK OF
NEWYORK , BARCLAY BANK , CITIGROUP , CITIBANK ...ETC SO WE CAN NOT USE OUR CREDIT CARTS OR TO PAY CASE
ANYBOY.YOU KNOW THAT WE HAS ONLY BEEN " WATCHING EVENTS " SURVIVING ON THE GOODWILL OF OUR FRIENDS IN
KANO , WE WERE WAITING FOR THE FEDERAL GOVENMENT TO PAY OUR FATHER ENTITLEMENTS SO THAT WE CAN HAVE
SOMETHING TO SURVIVE WITH ...ETC.ALL PROPERTIES BELONGING TO MY FATHER GENERAL SANI ABACHA AND OUR
FAMILY HAD BEEN CONFISCATED THESE INCLUDE ALL OUR HOUSES AND VEHICLES AND OUR ACCOUNTS IN ALL BANKS OF
NIGERIA , AND FOREIGN ACCOUNTS ABROAD , WE HAVE NOW BEEN PLACED UNDER HOUSE ARREST IN OUR SOUTHEN
NIGERIAN HOUSE TOWN OF ABACHA AS FOLLOWS :P.O.BOX 5375 MAIDUGURI, MAIDUGURI 5375 Nigeria. OUR HOUSE
IN UNITED SATE AS FOLLOWS :12102 BENMORE DRIVE HOUSTON, TEXAS 77099United States .BUT IT IS CLOSED
NOW .

WE HAVE BEEN TRIED TO ABONDON MY COUNTRY TO ANOTHER COUNTRY FOR EXEMPLE UNITED STATE OR SPAIN TO ASK
FOR POLITICAL REFUGEES BUT WE HAVE ARREST BY UNIT FORECE IN INTERNATIONL AIRPORT ANY WANY , CURRENTLY
, MY MOTHER Mrs.MARYAM ABACHA IS ILL SHE LOST TWO HIS SONS IBRAHIM NOW DECEESED AND MOHAMMED NOW
INCARCERETED BECOME AN OBJECT OF PROBE IN THE UNITED STATES .

I WANT ONLY TO PROVE YOU THAT WE ARE REALLY FAMILY OF FORMER PRESIDENT OF NIGERIA GENERAL SANI ABACHA
AND WE ARE NOT THE NIGERIAN SCAM .

YOURS FAITHFULLY.
MR .ABBA ABACHA.

I couldn't stop myself from laughing at the corrections. It was lunch time, so I called Martin on his cell phone. I could hear logging equipment working in the background as we talked. "Hey, it's me."

"What's up?"

"The Africans re-did the math and took the total up a notch to what I figured it to be. Twelve billion in various countries around the world, and then there is that other ten billion in the hands of some Arabic country."

Martin laughed. "Bigger dreams yet."

"Guess what?" I teased. "There is no money."

"Damn! Wish this weren't a scam."

"Ah but!" I exclaimed. "They told me emphatically that they are not 419 men."

"They've got big balls, my friend." Martin warned, "Be careful."

A problem arrived with Canada's Mr. Anthony Smith. No one ever answered his phone. Worst yet, when I called his bank, his name did not appear on the employee register.

That confirmed one thing: I had to make solid contact with the people in London and Amsterdam.

My next two attempts at making telephone contact in both locations were very successful. It was as if someone higher up put the word out for everyone to get back to work.

In my successful attempt to reach Mr. Dongote in London by phone, he said, "Yes, Mr. Wizard. I am sorry I have not been able to answer your calls. I have been out of the country. I am now back in London. I await your arrival."

"I can make plans to meet you as soon as possible?" I asked.

"Please. Come very soon. Let us get the details completed and the money into your account," Dongote told me.

"Fine. I'll book a flight today," I assured him.

Next, Dr. Samuel in Amsterdam answered his phone. "Please, Mr. Wizard, come to Amsterdam as soon as possible. Let us get the details completed and the money transferred to your account."

"I'll book the flight today," I repeated my line.

"Hmmm," I hummed, after hanging up. "They must read from the same script."

I was lucky enough to book a seat on the Virgin Atlantic flight to London the following week. That gave me a few days to pack my life into storage, then drive south to San Francisco.

I sent these two notes to Abba and Emma:

Mohammed K Abacha,1/26/00 10:26 PM -0700,Re: update.

```
        To: "Mohammed K Abacha" <mohammed.abacha@eudoramail.com>
      From: Brian Wizard <bwizard@eoni.com>
   Subject: Re: update.
        Cc:
       Bcc:
X-Attachments:
```

Mr. Abacha,
        You must contact me immediately, as I am about to depart from my office and head to Europe. As I explained yesterday, the journey rests on several counts: All I am bringing is a pen to sign paperwork that will release the money to me. There will be no fee payments on my part. This is to assure me that this is not a scam. I am only willing to receive the allocation of money from you.
        I would like to point out that you said only you and your brother know of this money, yet you give me a list of names of other people who handle the arrangements for payment. They all know everything.
        Anthony Smith, from what I have found out in my research, does not exist. He does not work at either bank in Toronto, of which you gave me phone numbers. No one has ever heard of him. Therefore, I wonder how this fake fellow will contact me.
        The D&L clearance certificate you asked me to pay for at the cost of $15,500 US is one of the certificates I have bought from the fake fellow, your words, Mohammed and his cohort David. It only cost $200. I only have a faxed copy of it, which I doubt will impress anyone.
        The deal in Spain is a no show at this point. No word from your man Mr. Roger Philips, or Philip Rogers.
        I have an airline ticket to London on hold at this moment. I have related business in Amsterdam, too. Am I going to Toronto, or London? Or Spain? I am ready to positivly conclude this business in your favor, but on my terms. All I am offering you is my signature and post-transaction investment assistance. Do you want it? If you are not running the Nigerian 419 scam then that is all you will want. Words mean little, action means everything.
        You mention there is danger and risk. I explained that you have me going into a situation blind, unarmed, with no back up, no medical assurance, no legal attention, no bail. This is a worry. I've done such things before and as I said, it simply makes the work harder. And, I usually get paid something up front. I would think that Mr. Dongote and his cohort Mr. Hamza would be able to send me a retainer, earnst money of $10,000, which will be given back after the transaction.
        So my friend, the ball is back in your court and you need to kick that sucker in the appropriate direction for me to make the goal.
                        Ready to rock and roll,
                        Brian Wizard

PS: If you have contact with any of the people you have working with you on this you might mention that I don't respond well to anger and hositility, as I have had to listen to recently in my phone conversations with London. I prefer the red carpet treatment and complete respect. My pen is ready to sign. Make it happen with trust and respect and we will all be happy.

Brian Wizard
P.O.Box 42
Wallowa, Or. 97885 USA
541 886 0119   (tele/fax)

1/26/00

Dr. Johnnson,

I have arrangements being made to fly to Europe next week. Before I confirm the expense of the ticket and hotel accommodations I will need a truthful word from you about the transaction you want me to conclude in Amsterdam. What I need to know is:

Exactly what will be expected from me: timewise

> financially
> professionally
> what risks will there be
> what paperwork will you expect me to have
> what paperwork will you provide to me at your expense
> what fees will I be expected to pay

I am expected to be in Viet Nam Feb 11, so I won't have but a day or so to conclude the business. I will be up-front with you and tell you that I will NOT pay any fees for any paperwork, etc. It is my opinion that at this time in the conclusion of your business proposal that I am the key element. I am willing to cover my transportation and lodging costs, but that is all. All other financial expenses, fees, etc. will have to be your party's. Please assure me that this is true.

I will leave here mid-next week for two or three days in London, then on to Amsterdam. I will need the contact number and addresses of whom I am to meet and where before I depart here.

Please assure me that all you will need from me is my signature and no cash outlay.

I await your immediate response.

Brian Wizard

Once I arrived in the Bay Area I arranged to stay at a friend's house north of the city. He said I could park my van there while I was out of the country. My friend, known mostly by his CB handle, the Fox, and I go back a long way. He sat with his eyes bulged with amazement as he listened to the details of my latest investigation. His good ear tilted my way so that he didn't miss a word.

"You taking any weapons?" was his first question, as he perused the African paperwork.

"My travel agent warned me, 'No firearms!'" I reported.

The Fox's face grimaced. "I'd love to give you some back up on this one, but I'm so broke I can barely afford rice and beans."

"I've got two knifes, one fold-up and one straight-bladed. I also have this," and I fished out my latest acquisition. A little something I picked up at a pawn shop. I handed a black, three-edged dagger-like implement to the Fox.

"A CIA letter opener," the Fox said with approval in his voice. "This should escape all electronic detection devices."

From an internet cafe' I faxed a note to Dr. Emma:

Brian Wizard
P.O.Box 42
Wallowa, Or. 97885

Dr. Johnson,
I have a flight to Europe for Tuesday. I will Arrive in London Wednesday. My business there will take a few days. I will head to Amsterdam as soon as I can to conclude our business. Please contact me soon to confirm this and answer the questions I asked in my last fax. I especially need to know the timing involved so I can continue my European business trip, and arrange the flights. I need to hear from you ASAP. If by chance there is no business for me to conclude in Amsterdam, please say so, preventing me from wasting any time .

Yours truly,

The cafe' also provided incoming fax service. I called Debbie and asked her to check my e-mail. "If anything comes in from any of the Africans, print it and fax it to me here," I instructed.

* * *

The clock was ticking, and time was moving at an accelerated speed, or so it seemed. The next day brought the final countdown to departure under twenty-four hours. I felt the same as I had thirty-odd years ago when I waited for the airlift that would take me to the fray of combat in Viet Nam. I had unlimited arms and ammo, plus massive backup that time. This time I was going into combat against a small contingent of Nigerian scamsters blind, unarmed, with no backup, no medical rescue or financial bail out. I was ready to dance straight into the weird world of the scam. My combat-ready lamp continued to glow with its cautionary pale yellow.

I relaxed for a moment when I found three faxes waiting for me at the internet cafe'. One was from Dr. Emma, and two from Abba, relayed by Debbie.

DR. EMMA JOHNSON BSC., ICAN., MBA.,Ph.D.

EXECUTIVE CHAIRMAN
CONTRACT AWARD COMMITTEE (NNPC)
IKOYI - LAGOS NIGERIA
TEL/FAX: 234-90-405410

January 28, 2000

Dear Dr. Wizard,

I have received your faxes of 26 and 27, Jan. 2000.

In a nutshell, we have completely done everything at this end to have the Fund paid to you. Your own is to go to Amsterdam as advised to sign the Fund releasing documents.

There is not much expected of you. Ordinarily you should have your passport or National ID for identification purpose.

I am very happy that you are learned, experienced and well exposed, hence, use your common sense and discretion, if there is any other thing more than this, and let me know immediately.

I wish you safe journey to Europe and please keep in touch with me wherever you are, all the times.

Regards, **Dr. Emma Johnson**

It was good to read the fax from Dr. Emma. His statement declaring that all I needed to do in Amsterdam was sign some papers made me feel comfortable. Of course, that stimulated the question: Is this a real scam, or not? Followed by: When will Interpol intervene?

Don't worry. I had my rap down as to the how and why I was doing what I was doing, if the police were ever to show up. I had my business cards ready for distribution. *Brian Wizard: Investigative Novelist.* My opening statement would be, "What took you so long?"

If I did receive a large chunk of money, you know I would do the right thing: Work it, baby. Work it!

There is one thing I personally consider a crime, and that's dead money. Money left lying around in savings accounts. I'm not negating the value of a financial buffer to cover the hard times. My complaint is with the hoarding of large sums of money. Money has only one purpose. Spend it! Yes, that includes investments. Looted funds stashed in banks around the world are the greatest financial crime. That's where I came in. I would put the money back into circulation.

I read the other two faxed e-mail messages.

Mohammed K Abacha, 1/28/00 5:12 AM -0700, FW. 1

```
X-From_: mohammed.abacha@eudoramail.com  Fri Jan 28 04:13:22 2000
To: bwizard@eoni.com
Date: Fri, 28 Jan 2000 04:12:44 -0800
From: "Mohammed K Abacha" <mohammed.abacha@eudoramail.com>
Mime-Version: 1.0
Cc: bwizard@eoni.com
X-Sent-Mail: off
Subject: FW.
X-Sender-Ip: 194.204.195.72
Organization: QUALCOMM Eudora Web-Mail  (http://www.eudoramail.com:80)

ATTN :-MR.BRIAN WIZARD.

I HAVE RECEIVED YOUR LAST A LETTER AND I HOPE YOU A GOOD TRIP TO LONDON BUT  STOP CONTACT WITH
Mr.ANTHONY SMITH UNITEL NEXT MARCH .
```

KEEP IN TOUCH WITH FOR ANY DEVELOPPMENT, AND
PLEASE DON'T FORGET TO SEND ME ALL DOCUMENTS VIA E-MAIL ATTACHMENT.

I LOOK FORWARD TO HEARING FROM YOU .

YOURS FAITHFULLY.

MR.ABBA ABACHA.

Mohammed K Abacha,1/28/00 10:11 AM -0700,Good...

```
X-From_: mohammed.abacha@eudoramail.com  Fri Jan 28 09:12:31 2000
To: bwizard@eoni.com
Date: Fri, 28 Jan 2000 09:11:48 -0800
From: "Mohammed K Abacha" <mohammed.abacha@eudoramail.com>
Mime-Version: 1.0
Cc: bwizard@eoni.com
X-Sent-Mail: off
X-Expiredinmiddle: true
Subject: Good...
X-Sender-Ip: 194.204.253.206
Organization: QUALCOMM Eudora Web-Mail  (http://www.eudoramail.com:80)
```

ATTN:-MR.BRIAN WIZARD.

I HOPE TO E-MAIL ME ALL DOCUMENTS BEFORE YOUR TRIP TO LONDON , DUE TO THE LARGE SUM OF AVAILABE FUNDS
INVOLVED AT THE SECURITY COMPANIES IN LONDON ,I ADVISE YOU TO ASK YOUR BANK IN UNITED STATE TO OPEN
FOR YOU ONE OR TWO DIFFERENT CURRENT ACCOUNTS WITH BARCLAYS BANK OR CITIBANK BRANCHES IN LONDON .MY
REASON FOR ADVISING YOU OF THIS IS DUE TO THE FACT THAT THE FUNDS NEED TO BE MOVED AROUND WITHEN THE
ACCOUNTS FIRST ,BEFORE IT CAN EVENTUALLY BE TRANSFERRED TO YOUR FORWARDED ACCOUNT IN UNITED STATE OF
AMERICA, REQUIREMENTS WILL FACILITATE THE IMMEDIATE EXECUTION OF THE TRANSACTION AS SOON AS POSSIBLE .

MYSELF AND MY MOTHER MARYAM ABACHA GIVE YOU THE BEST WISHES TO ALL MEMBERS OF YOUR FAMILY.AND I HOPE A
GOOD LUCK IN YOUR TRIP, ALWAYS KEEP ME POSTED AND GET BACK TO ME WITH BRIEFS OF THE PROGRESS IN
ARRANGING TO PICK UP THE FUNDS FROM THEIR VAULT.

BEST REGARDS.

MR.ABBA ABACHA.

I detected a hidden agenda coming into play with Abba's advice to open several bank accounts. I couldn't see how playing that game would make a difference. "Just send me the money," I told his fax.

I wasn't confident that Abba didn't expect me to pay some up-front fees. I sent him this e-mail from the cafe'.

Abba,
I am not, I repeat, NOT expected to pay any fees for this transaction.
Correct?
What about some earnest money to help defray the cost of my journey?
On the road,
Brian Wizard

HANDS-ON
ENGAGEMENT ONE

With the combat-ready lamp now glowing an amber yellow, I was living the combat rule of engagement: Get ready and stay ready.

Medicated with beer, good food, and the Fox's entertaining company, I managed to relax. Not an over indulgence, I simply took off some of the edge, lowered the hype, calmed the nerves. Okay, dulled the nerves. With my drag-along suitcase on wheels packed, my ticket and passport secured, I was ready. I had cash, credit cards, life insurance and a hotel room waiting for me in London. I even had my new Stetson hat brushed, shaped, and ready for wear. "The London fog, you know," I told the Fox, as I stood in front of his full-length dining room mirror and watched myself curl the sides of the brim one more time.

Life insurance was going to keep my estate going if I didn't make it back. I thought about medical insurance, as mentioned in the travel advisory to Benin. "Maybe I'll check on medical/flight insurance at the airport," I told the Fox.

"Good idea," he concurred. "Put me down as beneficiary."

"Will do, Captain. You get all the unpaid bills," I joked.

The Fox delivered me to the airport bus. For eighteen bucks one way I could travel the awkward eighty miles to the airport without inconveniencing anybody, most likely the Fox, for a ride. This would have meant two trips through, or around, the city of San Francisco for him. Not a fun drive, especially for the Fox, since he had lost both legs and a hand in combat in Viet Nam.

Boarding the bus brought back memories of the time I took a similar first step toward combat in the late sixties. That time the bus took me to the airport for an extended trip to Viet Nam. Both times held one thing in common: An unknown future.

I shook the Fox's hand and snapped him a salute as I boisterously said, "Game on!"

With some time to kill at the airport, I found the travel insurance I considered buying. Forty-five dollars bought a ten-day policy of death and medical coverage. The policy offered a lost baggage claim, too. I took it.

The life insurance part of the policy didn't mean that much. It was the medical insurance I wanted. Just in case I ended up with a gunshot wound, or a knife puncture, or laceration. I wasn't predicting a violent confrontation, yet the reality was I would soon be negotiating with an international gang of scamsters whose main intention was to rip me off. Then there was the accident-waiting-to-happen feature of Britain's contradictory-to-America's direction of road traffic.

Boarding the airplane felt the same as climbing aboard an assault helicopter for immediate delivery to the frontline. There was only one rule of engagement to live by at such a stage of transition: Enjoy the ride.

As I was getting seated on the plane, I neatly folded up the receipt for the insurance policy and filed it away in my carry-on bag. I always try to get a seat next to an emergency exit. I'm the kind of guy everyone on aboard would want next to the emergency exit door, as I can operate quite well under pressure. The best part, though, is that these seats usually provide extra leg space, since no seats block the emergency exits. I was happy to find that my request for an emergency exit seat had come through. I placed the bag and my Stetson hat in the overhead storage locker. I didn't need to see any of that stuff until we landed. All I needed was the book I bought to read, and my reading glasses.

The flight to London was quite entertaining. Virgin Atlantic didn't hold back when it came to keeping me well fed, watered, and mentally occupied.

Each seat had its own entertainment center, which included a small but adequate video screen. The video screen for my seat pulled up from the side on a multi-jointed arm. Each screen had separate controls. No more straining your neck to look over or around the seats between you and the sparingly place monitors of old. There were six movie channels, several TV channels, and one channel that displayed an animated map that followed the airplane's flight path.

With my shoes off and my legs outstretched, I was comfortable. There are a few more tricks I've picked up over the years that make long flights more comfortable, but I think it's best I keep them to myself. Otherwise, I wouldn't be the only one to receive the special attention.

My travel agent had assured me that once I hit London I'd be able to wing it. She has arranged travel for me to many places. Most destinations lacked the intricate network of transport and accommodations that London had to offer. My travel agent was right. I went from Heathrow Airport to Paddington on a non-stop underground rail line. I had a room reserved at the Quality Inn in Paddington. I walked out of the train station at Paddington and asked a cabby for a ride. He laughed when I told him my destination. "Let me save you a quid, mate. That's just around the corner." I walked to the hotel. London is expensive. I immediately realized I didn't have a large enough budget to party too many nights in this town. This was a strictly business visit.

By early afternoon, I was comfortable and relaxed in my hotel room. By six in the evening, I had slept a few hours, showered and been updated on the local weather and news by a television that had no sound control.

By seven in the evening, I was ready to probe the enemy lines. I wanted to make some contact. I stretched to loosen my muscles, and took in some deep breaths of air. Alert and ready, I placed my first call.

"Is Dongote there?" I asked the deep-voiced receptionist who answered the phone.

"Who is calling?" the familiar Nigerian-accented voice asked.

"Brian Wizard," I responded.

"Dongote is not here," the man told me. "He will be here later tonight."

"He should be expecting me," I told the receptionist.

"Yes, he is. I see your name on his appointment book," the receptionist confirmed. "He will talk to you tomorrow. Call again in the morning. You are in London now?"

"Yes, I am. That's why it is imperative that we connect tomorrow. I will only be in town a couple of days."

"Yes, I understand. We will begin the process tomorrow morning. Call at nine o'clock."

Disconnected, I sat back and tried to feel out the situation on the other end of the phone. Was it hostile in any way? No. That felt good.

"Now what?" I asked the familiar image starring back at me from the wall-mounted mirror. "Let's take a walk, eat some food, meet and greet the people?"

"Let's go," my image replied.

I began my reconnaissance of the Paddington area of London in my usual recon method: an ever-expanding spiral from the center of my newly established base camp. I spiraled counterclockwise through the maze of Paddington's streets. The sidewalks, the streets, the buildings, as well as all the cars, and buses, glistened from a saturating mist of rain.

A few blocks out into the wetness of this London night and I called myself stupid for not wearing my Stetson, or carrying my umbrella. "Next time, wear the rain gear, or stay inside," I told myself, running my fingers through my wet hair.

I noticed a breakfast cafe' within the first block. I calculated the chances were good that I would be sitting inside that restaurant in the morning. A few blocks along the rain intensified. I ducked into a Thai restaurant with chicken satay on my mind.

After the meal and a beer, my hair was still wet. Outside, the rain's intensity had not diminished. My walk back to the hotel was brisk.

At six the next morning I woke to the sound of trucks just outside my window. My internal clock was doing its best to readjust. I could have used more sleep, but a rush of adrenaline set me in motion. After all, it isn't every day I get to negotiate a deal with international scamsters. I did some stretching. I took another walk. I walked by the breakfast cafe' without stopping. My appetite had not yet adjusted and breakfast didn't feel right at that time. "Later," I told myself.

The streets were still shiny with rain. The sky was gray, and misty. My Stetson sat snugly upon my head.

On my mind was the upcoming phone call to Dongote. Eight-thirty was close enough to nine for me, and the flock of butterflies that fluttered around in my stomach, to make the call.

I recognized the same slow and deep voice when the receptionist answered my call.

"Is Dongote there?" I asked.

Obviously, the man on the phone recognized my voice, too. "Mr. Wizard. You will need to speak with the payment officer, Mr. Hamza. He is expecting your call. Call him now at 44 . . ." and he gave me Mr. Hamza's number.

"To whom am I presently speaking?" I asked.

"Mustapha," the man told me.

"Any relationship to the Mustapha who is in prison with Mohammed Abacha?" I interrogated. It was time to make it clear that I was aware of the situation in Nigeria. I wanted Mustapha to understand that I expected his complete assistance in closing this deal.

"No," he stated. "I am no relation to that man." Mustapha then instructed, "Call me back as soon as you have spoken with Mr. Hamza."

Before I called Hamza, it occurred to me that I had heard both names before. I flipped through my paperwork and found the source of the reference: The Nigerian newspapers. Both names belonged to one man, Hamza Mustapha. The man incarcerated with Mohammed Abacha on charges of murder and rape.

I called Hamza.

"Hello," a voice not so deep, yet definitely Nigerian in accent, spoke.

"Mr. Hamza? Brian Wizard. I've come to close a business transaction for Mohammed Abacha." That had to be a good introduction, I thought.

"Mr. Wizard, where have you been? We have spent too much time chasing you around," Hamza scolded.

"What are you talking about?" I retorted. "I just got here."

I guessed Hamza had confused me with someone else, or this impatience was some sort of ploy to keep me off guard. He toned down his irritation with me, and continued, "You have all the papers needed for this transaction?"

"I'm not sure. What papers do you expect me to have?"

"I will send my assistant to meet with you this afternoon. If he sees everything is in order, then we can proceed tonight."

"That sounds good to me. We only have a couple of days to pull this thing together," I warned.

"We can do this transaction this week. It won't take long." Hamza assured me.

After hanging up, I admitted to my mirrored reflection, "Nope. It won't take long to realize I'm a man with no money."

I called Mustapha. "Hamza said we should meet this afternoon."

"Stay at the hotel. Mr. Wizard," Mustapha told me.

"I might go for a walk, see some sights, you know? I didn't come all this way to stare at the four walls of a hotel room. When will you be here?"

"Call me at two this afternoon. I will meet with you soon after that," Mustapha assured me.

"It appears I'm getting the old run around," I told my reflection, after the call.

"Don't let the buggers wear you down," my reflection advised.

I took another shower. I took another nap. I watch more British TV. The British sit-coms, news, commercials and programming in general were no better, or worse, than those found in the states. I had more than a dozen channels to chose from, but none with anything worth watching. Luckily, I did receive CNN. I stayed abreast of the day's repeated news stories. Perhaps they'd have some news on the latest Nigerian scam attempt.

To kill more time I called the front desk to ask, "Can you bring me up a different TV? This one has no sound control."

The hotel maintenance man was soon at my door. Upon his departure, I had no TV at all.

Finally, two o'clock came and I made my call to Mustapha.

Mustapha answered promptly. "I'll be at your hotel within the half hour."

"I'll wait for you in the lobby," I told him.

I sat in every chair in the lobby at least once while I waited. I paced back and forth between the front doors and the bar. I went back to my room, my bunker, simply for something to do. I was happy to find the maintenance man in my room. He had brought a new television set and was hooking it up. I returned to the lobby.

While pacing around the lobby, I kept one eye on the doorway. There was a small hall between the inner hotel front door and the front door on the street. Glass windows allowed me to watch the doorways. No one could get in without walking through the little hallway. I was sitting on the inside front window sill when I first saw him. Moving with the grace of a gazelle, Mustapha swayed his large body through the small hall. His flowing strut into the lobby was one of confidence. The well-dressed, black Nigerian projected the very image I had imagined. He was tall and well built. He wore an expensive suit, but that only enhanced his gangster

117

image. His face and head held almost no hair. He removed the wrap-around sunglasses as he scanned the room for his prey.

I didn't move until we had made eye contact, and I knew that he knew I was his quarry. On our mutual approach in the middle of the lobby, I extended my right hand. He took it. In his grip I felt a lightness. I had expected a strong grip from such a big man. I wondered if he understood that the handshake meant neither of us was carrying weapons? I then led him into the bar. It was vacant, so we had privacy.

A quick check on my internal combat-ready lamp gave me no reason to advance to red: Danger.

I offered, "Want a beer, coffee, soda?" Even though no one was tending bar, I had it arranged with the front desk to serve drinks to anyone with whom I met.

"No, thank you," Mustapha declined. "We need to talk about you and your business plans for this money."

"Fine. What do you want to know?"

"Have you run million- dollar transactions through your bank account before? We don't want to raise any eyebrows if the bank is suspicious of any large deposits into your account," Mustapha explained.

"I do one thing really well with money," I confidently told him, "and that is move money around. I play the stock market, make movies, buy and sell real estate, open and close businesses. The bank works hard keeping up with my money transactions. They won't bat an eye."

In actuality, I've never had more than fifty grand in any account, any-where, at any one time. What would Mustapha know about that? Nothing. That's real information. In the weird world of the scam we trade in lies, not the truth.

"Good," Mustapha praised. "How will you work this money?"

"Work it? Man, I've got a million investments waiting for an influx of money. Just tell me your interests. The stock market, perhaps? I have three accounts. Want to make some movies? Want to buy some real estate?

"I believe the best bang for the buck would come in the development of a strip of land in Nevada. It has two gambling saloons, a hotel and a trailer park. It could be turned into a gold mine. It's Nevada! Know what I mean?"

Mustapha didn't know what I meant. He just nodded his head in approval.

"I'll sit on your money, if you want. I'll put it into bank CDs, if that feels safer to you. Well, your share. My share I will put to work immediately." I couldn't help myself from grinning. Even though this was all BS on a grandiose scale, the excitement I generated by telling my plans made me ready to take immediate delivery of a few million bucks.

Silence fell between us for a moment. I wondered if I met Mustapha's standard of greed and gullibility. I asked, "So, what does it take to get started? I have a time limit."

"The payment officer will meet with you tonight," Mustapha told me.

"Hamza?"

"Yes. Mr. Hamza. Call him at the number I gave you this morning at seven o'clock tonight. He will arrange to meet with you here."

"Okay," I said slowly, showing my disappointment. "How long will this transaction take? I came early so that we don't get hung up over the weekend."

"We should be done by Friday night," Mustapha predicted.

Mustapha left. As I watched him gracefully walk away, I thought, "Hmmm, things went well." I made a mental review of what had just happened. I remembered seeing a cell phone hanging on Mustapha's belt. If all phone calls were to a cell phone, and these guys have no fixed address, then I'd have no recourse if anything went wrong. I saw the light. It shone directly on the core of the scam. Take the money and run. My gut feeling told me Mustapha's job was to size me up for the kill. Later tonight they'd hit me with the nitty-gritty of the genuine fake deal.

Before he was out of sight from my vantage point at the hotel's front window, I decide to follow him. A car's license plate number would give me information that could lead to a fixed address. It would be a way of tracking him down.

Luckily, due to my recon of the area the night before, I had a fair idea of which way he would go, especially if he was traveling by subway or train. I followed him by walking toward Paddington Station. To my surprise, I had lost him by the time I turned the second corner. I saw no one matching the tall black man's body, head or gait. I looked inside the vehicles on the street. Nothing. I thought about running to see if I could catch up to him. I then noticed I was standing in front of the breakfast cafe'. Hard investigating with a hands-on attitude makes me hungry. To hell with following Mustapha. "Let's eat," I told my blurred reflection starring back at me from the rain-wet glass of the restaurant's front door.

Unbelievable! There sat Mustapha at the third table, facing the door. He nodded in recognition after our eyes met. I guessed that working the scam also stimulates an appetite. I went over to his table. "Mind if I join you?"

"Not at all. Hungry?" Mustapha asked.

"I came for breakfast."

"Order whatever you want. I will pay for it," Mustapha offered.

"Thanks."

We shot the breeze while we ate. I brought up the topic of Mohammed's health. Mustapha laughed when I told him I heard Mo was getting sicker by the minute.

"They are using every trick in the book to get him released from that prison," he informed me with confidence.

I asked, "If I went to Nigeria would I have a good time?"

"Certainly," Mustapha assured. "Nigeria has everything you want."

"Beautiful women?"

"Many beautiful black women."

Through our chat, it became obvious to me that other than the scam and a mutual desire for easy money, we had little in common. Mustapha didn't have many outside interests. No music. No artwork. No hobbies. None that he cared to discuss, anyhow.

With breakfast under my belt, and my first hands-on scam contact in London well underway, it was time to set things up in Amsterdam. I called Dr. Samuel. He was right there to answer the phone.

"I'll be in Amsterdam sometime this weekend," I informed him. "Can we meet on Monday?"

"Yes, Mr. Wizard. Monday will be fine. Call me Monday morning and we'll arrange a meeting," Dr. Samuel advised.

I called around town using the yellow pages as my guide. I bought a round trip ticket to Amsterdam on British Midland, a local airline. The price of a round trip ticket was ninety-four pounds. Not bad. I was to depart London at one o'clock Saturday afternoon. This gave me a mere two days to work the London scam. Time was running quickly to its end.

I called Martin's wife, Debbie. She said she'd monitor my e-mails and snail mail and pay bills for me. "Anything come in from Africa?" I asked.

"Yes, there is," she told me in an upbeat tone. "Several e-mails."

"Would you be so kind as to print them out, attach them all to one page and fax that page to me?"

You have to love today's high-speed communications network. I had one fax containing four e-mails from Abba within the hour. One of the first things I noticed was the way Abba had changed his name. On the first e-mail he had signed off with Abba. The rest he signed with a more formal rendition: Abdulkadir Abacha. The last fax was different yet when he added a hyphen to Abdul-kadir.

Mohammed K Abacha,5/30/00 7:27 AM -0700,Re: Update. 1

```
From: "Mohammed K Abacha" <mohammed.abacha@eudoramail.com>
Mime-Version: 1.0
Cc: bwizard@eoni.com
X-Sent-Mail: off
Subject: FW.
X-Sender-Ip: 194.204.195.72
```

ATTN:-MR.BRIAN WIZARD.
        WELL,YOU ARE NOT GOING TO PAY ANY FEES YOU ARE GOING TO PICK UP THE FUNDS IN THEIR VAULT ,I WAS ASKED YOU TO SEND ME VIA E-MAIL ATTACHMENT,THE CERTIFICATE OF OWNERSHIP AND DRUG CLEARANCE CERTIFICATE, AND CERTIFICATE FOR OPEN AN ACCOUNT ON lIBERAL BANKING LAWS AND YOUR IDENTIFICATION AND YOUR PICTURE.
        Mr.DANGOTE WILL BE HAND YOU IN LONDON THE FILE ALL CERTIFICATES FOR FUNDS DEPOSITED IN SOUTH KORIA AND AUSTRALIA AND DENMARK AND HOLLAND AND ALSO IN GERMANY AND SWITZERLAND.
        Mr.ROGERS WILL BE HAND YOU IN MADRID THE FILE ALL CERTIFICATES FOR THE FUNDS DEPOSITED IN CANADA,UNITED STATE ,GANA ,IVORY COAST AND SOUTH AFRICA.
        I HOPE YOU A GOOD TRIP. .
BEST REGARDS.
MR.ABBA ABACHA.

ATTN:-MR.BRIAN WIZARD.
        WELL ,YOU SHOULD CONTACT ME IMMEDIATLY AT MY TOP SECURITY PHONE FOR ABACHA'S FAMILY. +234-1-775 1569. +234-1-774 5439.
        YOU CAN STOP OR CANCELLING THIS BUSINESS IF YOU ARE AFRAID SO FREEZE IMMEDIATLY FURTHER COMMUNCTATION WITH MR.DANGOTE AND MR.ANTHONY SMITH AND MR.ROGER. YOU REFUSE ALL MY LAST EXPLIAN TO YOU I TELL YOU AS YOU LIKE, I WAS EXPLIAN YOU THAT WE ARE NOT SCAM BUT WE ARE ABACHA'S FAMILY WE NEED AN ASSISTANCE IN OVERSEAS BUT YOU ARE NOT BELIEVE US, AND I TOLD YOU TO SEND ME YOUR DOCUMENTS BUT YOU REFUSE IT ANYWAY AS YOU LIKE .
        YOURS FAITHFULLY.
        MR.ABDULKADIR ABACHA BROTHER OF FORMER HEAD OF STATE GENERAL SANI ABACHA.

ATTN :-MR.BRIAN WIZARD .

PLEASE DON'T ANGRY ABOUT ME .PLEASE CALL ME IMMEDIATLY TO TALK WITH ADOUT THE FUNDS ANYWAY I WILL TRANSFER FOR YOU SWISS ACCOUNTS 20.000 $ AS EXPENSES FOR YOUR TRIP .MY PHONE IS : +234-1-7745439.

MR .ABDULKADIR ABACHA.

```
ATTN:-MR.BRIAN ABACHA.
         WELL,I HAVE RECEIVED YOUR LETTER AND I HOPE SO THAT YOU CAN UNDERESTAND ME. ANYWAY,I WILL BE
SENDING YOU THE MONEY TO COVER YOUR EXPENSES FROM MY OWN ACCOUNTS BANK IN SWITZERLAND " Union Bank of
Switzerland ,Rue du Mont-Blanc 28/Place de Cornavin 12 1201 Genhve.Tele:+41-22-375 33
47/Telefax:+41-22-375 33 37.
         I AM ABDUL-KADIR YOUNGER BROTHER OF FORMER HEAD OF STATE GENERAL SANI ABACHA ,Mrs .MARYAM (
SANI ABACHA'S WIDOW ) WHO IS REQUISTED YOU TO SEND YOUR DOCUMENTS TO US VIA E-MAIL ATTACHMENT YOU MUST
SEND IT IMMEDIATLY AND DON'T TRAVEL TO LONDON AND STOP FURTHER COMMUNECTION WITH MR.DANGOTE AND HIS
COLLEAGUES AND WITH MR.ANTHONY,DON'T SEND HIM ANY FEES OR MONEY .
         YOU SHOULD CALL MR.ROGERS PHILIPS AT HIS OFFICE NOW ,AND KEEP IN TOUCH FOR ANY
DEVELOPMENT.AND I HOPE TO SEE THIS SITE WEB:
>
>http://cnn.com/WORLD/africa/9910/14/BC-CRIME-NIGERIA-ABACHA.reut/index.html
>
>http://www.africanews.org/west/nigeria/stories/19981115_feat1.html
>
>http://cnn.com/WORLD/europe/9910/14/BC-SWISS-ABACHA.reut/index.html
>
>http://cnn.com/WORLD/africa/9910/13/nigeria.abacha.reut/index.html
>
>http://cnn.com/WORLD/africa/9910/13/BC-CRIME-NIGERIA-ABACHA.reut/index.html
>
>MR.ABDUL-KADIR ABACHA.
```

I did appreciate the first line of Abdul's first e-mail: "*. . . you are not going to pay any fees.*" That was not only what I wanted to hear, but that was exactly what I wanted in writing.

I didn't know where Dongote was. I hoped someone would hand me more paperwork that would allow me to pick up more money. They even had some in Holland. I could add that to my next trip.

Oh, yeah, I'd forgot. This was all a scam. Damn!

The second faxed e-mail message provided two security home phone numbers for Abba. I doubted they worked.

"I'm in the game now, partner," I said out loud after reading his suggestion that I had the opportunity to back out.

The third faxed e-mail message was weird. I didn't know why he thought I was angry at him. Nonetheless, hooray for the twenty grand in earnest money. "Damn!" I complained after reading how he was sending it to my non-existent Swiss account. I never told him I had such an account. That means he has no intention of sending me any money. Scamsters, they are so tricky.

The fourth message's greeting of, "*ATTN:-MR. BRIAN ABACHA.*" made me laugh. Now I'm part of the Abacha family, or Abba is getting confused as to who was who. The reiteration of forthcoming expense money sounded good, but the warning not to play with the bad boys in London was a bit late.

"Philips in Canada is on hold, my friend. First London. Then Amsterdam," I told the man as if he were in the room with me.

I did more milling about, seriously bored. Bored stupid. "Come on, seven o'clock," I commanded.

Finally seven o'clock arrived. I placed the call. "Hamza."

"Who is calling?" he asked.

"Brian Wizard, just like you instructed. Are we going to meet tonight?"

"No. Tomorrow morning. I will come to your hotel. Call me at ten in the morning."

"Oh, man," I complained to my reflection. "I hate all this waiting around."

With my internal clock reset, I awoke at sunrise, as per usual. I walked around my ever-expanding spiral, only this time clockwise. This part of Paddington was no more than a bedroom community. It had the odd mom and pop stores on every block that offered snacks, fruits, newspapers and magazines, and a varying assortment of sundry merchandise.

I bought a newspaper and went to the breakfast cafe'. I took a seat at the last table against the rear wall. It's a security thing. I could see everyone who walked into the restaurant, and none could walk behind me. I set my Stetson on the inside chair, looked up, and fell in love, or at least into a serious case of lust.

The waitress was absolutely stunning. Her shape was perfect. I watched her reach to a top shelf, for what I don't know, as all my eyes could see was the most beautiful woman on earth stretched tall and long, slender and most desirable. "Got to get to know you," I sang a part of an old song the name of which I couldn't remember. I watched her go about her business of waitressing. I admired every physical aspect of her person. She had long black hair. Jet black. Straight hair that hung past her shoulders. Her perfect complexion enhanced her radiant countenance. She had a mouth that I wanted to know up close and personal. Eyes I wanted to look deep into. A nose I could only imagine pressed hard against me in a deep sensual embrace. Every curve of her body complimented the next curve. I could not place her ethnic background. Perhaps Irish. Perhaps Mediterranean.

As she walked toward me, pen and paper in hand, looking right at me, I saw every sway of every curve. I fell into a dream that she was about to ask me to dance. A slow dance. A dance of love.

"Can I help you?" she asked.

"Will you marry me?" my heart blurted out, to my own surprise.

The waitress smiled. "Sorry. We aren't allow to marry our customers," she replied. Her accent was not British.

"Where are you from?" I asked.

"Ukraine," she told me.

I wanted to ask her every question ever asked just so she'd be close to me. I could see her expression change from friendly to suspicious. Every guy she waited on probably hit on her. The torment of natural beauty is a heavy social burden. I assumed she did not care to waste any more time listening to the gambit of inconsequential romance, again.

"Two scrambled eggs and toast."

"That comes with chips," she informed me.

"Chips, too," I agreed. I asked her, as she wrote my order, "Why are you a waitress and not a super-model?"

"I think waitress is a sure thing for making money. Modeling is difficult," she explained.

"I can't imagine anyone not wanting to pay you big money to model their clothes. You are the most beautiful woman I have ever seen. Ever."

She smiled, then walked away. I starred after her, hoping she'd come back. She did the next best thing. She looked over her shoulder at me, and smiled again. Sad to say, but that was the closest I had gotten to romance in years.

At ten I called Hamza. "We on for today?" I asked.

"Yes, Mr. Wizard. I should be at your hotel around one o'clock this afternoon."

"That late? Do you think we can conclude this business in just a few hours?"

"We can get the process started. We will conclude business shortly thereafter," Hamza predicted. "It depends on you."

"Me? Why me? You're the man in charge, Hamza. What can I do to conclude the process?"

"I will show you everything this afternoon," Hamza assured me.

"I'll be here."

More waiting. Only three hours. I finished reading the book I had bought for the airplane ride. I milled around the lobby, talking with the people at the front desk. I had fun hitting on Marie from Spain. It didn't take me long to bring the discussion around to the idea of her and me having some fun. Adult fun. "You could show me the town after work," I told her.

"I will be very tired," she told me, declining my offer.

"We could go to your house. I'll cook you a fine meal, while you relax in a hot bath. While the meal cooks, I will wash your back and massage your tired feet."

"No. I don't think so," she declined again.

Finally, at twelve-fifteen the butterflies stirred. I wanted some action. I couldn't believe this scam was more about wasting time than money.

My combat-ready lamp never turns red until there has been a true detection of a threat. Even though Mustapha looked the part of a gangster, he had never posed any real threat. He had seemed to be quite a pleasant man, really. Therefore, I remained calm as I waited in the lobby for Hamza.

One o'clock came and went. At one-thirty I called Hamza's number from my room. "Where are you?"

"About five minutes away, Mr. Wizard," Hamza said.

I had no doubt that he was talking on a cell phone. I listened to the background noise, but there was none. This must mean he was in a car. I returned to the hotel bar. It was devoid of customers. Good. I watched the large TV set up on a stand. It was a repeat of CNN news. The anchor could have tested me on any of the day's subjects, as I knew all the answers.

My peripheral vision detected movement in the lobby. Two black men, dressed for the part of gangsters, entered the hotel. I turned to the CNN anchor and announced, "This just in, Game on!" I turned off the television.

When I turned around, Mustapha walked into the bar, followed by the man who had to be Hamza, the payment officer. Hamza wasn't as big and buff as Mustapha. There was a third man missing. Dongote. Abba told me to meet with Dongote, who was to hand me paperwork for more transactions. I had never heard Mustapha or Hamza refer to him, other than he

125

wasn't available. Abba had never mentioned either of these two men. This I found suspicious.

Mustapha introduced Hamza to me. We moved to the only large table in the room. I studied Hamza. He had short, tightly curled hair on his head and clean-shaven cheeks, but sported a mustache and goatee. He wore an expensive looking suit, and carried a briefcase.

Our conversation started with a repeat of what Mustapha and I talked about earlier: My plans for the money. I also assured Hamza, "The bank will not be alarmed by this transfer. I move a lot of money through my account."

The game turned serious when Hamza placed the briefcase on the table. Mustapha scanned the lobby, then shot Hamza an "all clear" nod.

Hamza said to me, almost in a whisper, "This is why we are here." He opened the briefcase and revealed what appeared to be a lot of money. There were ten stacks of $100 U.S. bills wrapped in firm cellophane. Five stacks had a stain over Franklin's face. The other stacks did not have such a stain. Hamza began to weave his web of trickery.

"You see this stain?" he asked, pointing to one of the top one-hundred dollar bills.

I nodded affirmatively.

"This mark prevents the bills from being detected by security devices. It is not legal to transport such large sums of money across borders, as we have done," Hamza explained.

I had heard stories about the ink of money being made from metals, like copper, for detection by metal-sensitive devices. The theory had the potential of being true.

"Why aren't these stained?" I asked about the clear bills on top of five of the stacks.

"The bills underneath the top bills are stained," Hamza told me.

"Okay," I said, my tone denoting disbelief.

"This mark is removed by washing the bills with a special chemical solution. We buy this chemical in full strength, then dilute it," Hamza clarified. "The mark is washed from the money, then it is good for deposit into any bank."

This theory sounded good, to a point. This plot truly redefined the concept of laundered money. I shouldn't need a Clearance Certificate from

the National Drug Law Enforcement Agency. A receipt from a local laun-
dromat would seem sufficient. I almost laughed at my thoughts, but held
my face in an expression of curiosity and interest.

Hamza then made a play for my money. "This is where we have a
problem, Mr. Wizard. We are out of this chemical. We can buy more. We
have connections with a Mr. Smith who works for a bank. He will sell us
the chemical."

"Smith? Anthony Smith?" I interrupted. "The Smith from Canada?"

"No," Mustapha butted in, as if he knew Anthony Smith from Canada.

"Can you buy this chemical for us today, Mr. Wizard?" Hamza asked.

"Sure. Where do I go?"

"You give us the money. We will buy the chemical," Hamza offered.

I let out a sigh, sat back in my chair and starred at Hamza, then over to
Mustapha. To myself I thought, this is all you've got? You need my money
to buy chemicals to literally launder the money? I sat upright and moved
my butt to the edge of the chair. I studied the money in the briefcase. I saw
something off color. The top bills on the ten stacks looked like real money.
The paper underneath was too white to be real money. It looked more like
copy paper.

My actions must have been negative body language to Hamza. He
immediately ended his request for money to buy chemicals. "I don't want
to worry you about this problem. We can handle this ourselves. We have a
bigger situation that will need your attention."

Oh, boy, I thought. Here comes the clincher.

"We only have this one million dollars, at this moment. We have a new
shipment containing two million more ready to be picked up today. We
need to pay five-thousand pounds in order to pick up this shipment. This is
where you come in. You can speed this transaction along by making this
payment," Hamza explained.

A rough calculation made five thousand pounds about eight thousand
dollars, at that day's rate of exchange. If this was a true-to-life offer it
would be a bargain. For eight grand I would buy two million dollars? I
could live with that. Sold on the idea, I wasn't. It was a scam. The real
scenario would have been more like: I give them money. They disappear. I
would have nothing of any value to show for the transaction. They
probably wouldn't have given me a receipt.

"Can I open one of those packets? I want to flip through it," I ventured.

"No," Hamza stated. He shot a glance to Mustapha, who sat ready.

"When would you have the money?" I asked. "I'm on a tight schedule."

The fact was, I had seen enough. They had laid their cards on the table, and had nothing. I was ready to move on to Amsterdam. I worried that if these guys were to consider me trouble, or decide I was simply not acceptable material for the scam, they might call their cohorts in Amsterdam and warn them. Such a thing could spoil that end of the investigation. I needed at least two scam attempts for an honest evaluation.

On the other hand, it would be a good thing to know if these two scam factions were part of a collective network that made up a greater Nigerian Scam syndicate. Was there one boss? Were there seminars given to teach the scam to recruited operators? Did they have any type of security force? I remembered reading in the U.S.State Department Travel Advisory on the internet a mention of the scam and how one could lose his money, ". . .or *his life.*"

I decided to rub them the wrong way. I started with, "You know Abba, Abdulkadir Abacha?" Hamza's eyes lit up. I passed him the faxed e-mail I recently received. "This clearly states that I am not expected to pay any fees. How am I going to explain this to him?"

"Let me see that," Mustapha told Hamza. I suspected Mustapha was the better English reader of the two.

"I came to London with enough time to conclude business this week. I have another appointment to do the same sort of thing in Amsterdam on Monday. I can't hang around here waiting for you to buy chemicals and launder money, pardon my pun. What does that smudge do again?" I asked.

"It prevents detection," Hamza reported.

These guys needed a better script writer. Who would fall for this crap?

"Look at this," I told to Mustapha, as I handed him the e-mail from Abba that listed all the places where I could go pick up money, some with contact names and numbers. "You understand that I am working in close quarters with the Abacha family. I am not supposed to be hit up for fees. In fact," I pointed to the list of faxed e-mails, "you can read for yourself that Abba plans to send me twenty grand for expenses. I will be able to help you out after I receive his money."

"You can't collect all of this money," Mustapha told me, referring to the list I passed him.

I ignored his nay-saying, and told him, "I'm going to Amsterdam to pick up thirty-two million on Monday."

I turned to Hamza, and suggested, "We can call Abba right now. On your cell phone. He gave me his personal security line phone number. It's right here, see? Only in a case of emergency. This is an emergency."

"He has no security phones," Mustapha corrected me. "All his lines are tapped."

"He says they are secure. Let's call him," I encouraged.

"No. This is not right," Hamza told me. "You give us the five thousand pounds now. We will bring you the money tonight."

"What about washing off the smudges?" I asked.

"That will be taken care of," Hamza assured me.

"Do you have a physical address?" I inquired, through a serious poker face.

"Not for business, Mr. Wizard," Mustapha told me.

I leveled with them. "The way I see it, you have a briefcase full of paper, not money. If it is real, why do you need my money to buy chemicals to wash off the stains?" I asked them quite bluntly. My head involuntarily wagged negatively from left to right. "And you want me to pay up-front fees, against Abba's instructions. I can't do it."

Hamza sat in his chair, motionless. His face showed no particular emotion.

"Here's the best I can offer." I explained. "If and when I collect Abba's twenty grand, I'll come back. If the guys in Amsterdam come through as they said they would, I'll have extra cash. I'll call you Wednesday and let you know. Okay?"

"We cannot wait for you, Mr. Wizard," Hamza barked, sitting up straight, and irritated.

"Wednesday is not far off. I'll call you and let you know if I have any money. I can give you some then, as long as Abdulkadir gives me the go ahead." I felt in control.

"We must take delivery of the money soon. Call us Wednesday, but be assured that if something else comes up, we must move on it," Hamza explained.

I walked them to the hotel's front door. Soon, they were out of sight. I considered following them. I would have loved to get a license plate number. Then again, why should I? I watched what would have happened if I had given them any money: they were melding into the London populace, never to be seen by me again.

When I walked back into the hotel I noticed a strange look on the face of the front desk clerk. His expression was one of fear. "What?" I asked.

"Those guys were gangsters," he claimed.

"Scamsters," I corrected.

An hour later I called Hamza. The phone was busy.

I called Mustapha. His phone was busy, also.

"So much for the London operation," I told my reflection. "Let's party!"

While preparing for a stroll along the wet streets of London, I began to sing a part of the Beatles' *A Day In the Life*. "Grabbed my coat," but instead of, "grabbed my hat," I had to change the words to, "Couldn't find my hat."

"Hmmm," I hummed with perplexity. It was one of those moments when my memory failed me. What did I do with my hat? It was nowhere in sight. Running through my memory of the day's events as I would a photo album, I saw the last time I wore the hat. "Breakfast!" I could clearly see my hand placing the hat on the table's inside chair. I then remembered reaching to the top of my head after stepping outside and retrieving my reading glasses, but no hat.

The first stop on my night on the town was the breakfast cafe'. Of course, I wished that the waitress I saw earlier in the day would be there. She'd be out of her work clothes, wearing something hot and slinky. She'd be willing and ready to make a new best friend. She wasn't there. I looked on the seat, but no hat. I asked the waiter if anyone had turned in a hat. "I last saw mine here," and I pointed to the chair.

He looked in all the usual places employees put left-behind items. There was no hat.

"Oh well," I gave in to the reality that I had indeed lost my hat. Someone is looking good, I figured. I could only assume that the next customer to sit at the table found the hat, liked it, and wore it away. My consolation prize was the positive thinking: One less thing to carry.

I returned to my hotel room and picked up my umbrella. "What a good boy scout," I commended my reflection as I passed it by.

Back into the wet and dreary London night, I boarded the tube and rode it to Piccadilly Circus. No circus was in town. I hit a few pubs to knock back a couple of mood-enhancing beers. My eyes were as keen as a hawk's in search of prey. I wanted a woman to share some small talk with me. I thought that if this were a Hollywood movie, the waitress from the breakfast cafe' would walk right in front of me. She never did. Damn it! In fact, in my three-hour jaunt into the night life of London I never had one conversation with anybody. I kept an eye out for Mustapha, too. We could talk more about Mohammed's plight.

Too soon I was back in my hotel room and bored stupid. When I walked through the hotel lobby I heard the din of a crowd in the bar. I shook off the wet of the night air, then decided to journey to the bar to continue my hunt for some female companionship. I like the hunt.

I sat at the bar. I had already hit on the bartender for her affection the night before, but she had declined my offer. Lydia and I were just friends. A group of Germans surrounded the table where I met with Mustapha and Hamza. They seemed excited about something. Up close, their chatter was loud and boisterous.

"Ahhh, what's this?" I asked my reflection in the mirror behind a stock of liqueur bottles on the other side of the bar. In the reflection I saw two women and a man walk into the room. I remained seated. It was a small bar. The newcomers came to my left side. The man and one of the women sat at a small table, while the other woman took up a seat at the bar. Their speech told me right away that they were Aussies. Assessing the situation, I speculated that the man and woman at the table were a couple and the woman at the bar was the odd-person-out. I could only be so lucky.

"What brings you folks up and over to London," I asked them collectively.

"We're here for a trade show," the woman at the bar spoke up.

"What are you trading?" I inquired.

"We're in the rag trade."

"Rag trade? Old clothes?" I guessed.

"No. New fashions. We are all designers," the woman explained.

We talked for forty minutes. I told them about my dealings with the scam artists, and how it was my latest investigation. Amazingly enough, the guy

131

had once received a letter from West Africa that told him that he too was due a few million dollars.

What struck me funny was that the Aussies occasionally laughed at an inside joke. I didn't pick up on the humor right away. Then it came clear that every once in a while the guy would say something that would make the girls giggle. The joke had something to do with me. Something to the effect that he would like to hear about my adventure in a more private setting. I had to get to the bottom of this, no pun intended. I made my move on the woman at the bar.

"So, maybe those two would like some quality time together, and you and I could hang out? In my room, perhaps."

This made one thing clear. I had no sexual interest in men, but plenty in women. The woman sitting at the table with the man, said to him, "No luck for you tonight." She then turned to me and stated, "She's mine."

I saw the look of a jealous man in her eyes. "Yeah, right," I challenge. "You're saying this guy would go out with me, but neither of you ladies would?"

"You got it," the woman at the table told me.

"Wow," I said with disappointment. "That's weirder than anything the Africans ever told me." I turned to Lydia. "Looks like it's you and me tonight, my dear."

Lydia heard the conversation, smiled and encouraged me with, "Maybe."

*   *   *

In the end, I closed the hotel bar down with Lydia, but returned to my room alone. In my room, boredom, disappointment and an overall melancholy mood settle over me. I called Hamza, even though it was late. All I heard was a busy signal. I called Mustapha and received the same cold shoulder.

I called both Hamza and Mustapha again in the morning. Busy. That must be what you get in Britain when people turn off their cell phones. That is what would have happened had I given them one red cent, or more. They would have simply disappeared, leaving me no recourse. I could go to the police, but what would I tell them? "I got involved with a gang of scamsters and they ripped me off!" I don't think that would have been interesting enough to make a bobby walk out into the rain to help me.

Luckily, I had lost nothing. I was still under my four thousand dollar budget. A flutter of excitement ran through me as I realized my next adventure into the weird world of the scam would take place in Amsterdam. I could only hope Dr. Samuel had a better story.

BM British Midland
The Airline for Europe

```
                        PASSENGER  RECEIPT  1OF1                      O
                        05FEB00 91499273   SITI GB
           A44614VK    /LONDON LHR              ... /BMR
  /BMR                                      O
  **NOT VALID FOR**   **THIS IS YOUR RECEIPT**    LONDON LHR
  **TRANSPORTATION*                               BD 105 Q 05FEB  QXSS
VALID BD ONLY            NO CHANGES/REFUNDS       AMSTERDAM AMS
                              N257GP / BD         BD 112 Q 08FEB  QXSS
                                                  LONDON LHR

/FC 05FEB00LON BD AMS59.08 BD LON50.98 NUC110.06END ROE 0.617797SITIXT6.10RN2.60NL

                        FP CCVI446561090071 2957/0201/901115

GBP    68.00
  GB   10.00      ***************************  ********************
  UB    7.30                                   NOT VALID FOR TRAVEL
  XT    8.70           0 236 2107535415 5       236 2107535415 5
GBP    94.00
```

ENGAGEMENT TWO

I returned to the breakfast cafe' as giddy as a high school boy with romantic expectations. I sat at the same table as the day before. I tried not to let the super-model-waitress notice my magnetized stare. I couldn't help watching her every move. I had a newspaper to read. I was hoping that my reading glasses would hide my eyes. After she took my order, I asked if she had seen my hat. She hadn't. When I walked out of the cafe' for the last time, I gave her my card. "If you ever change your mind about marriage." I knew she never would, but at least I had done my best.

Back at the hotel I busied myself with packing. I kept my umbrella handy, inside my carry-on bag. Surprise came when I tilted my drag-along suitcase into its upright position to begin my journey to Amsterdam. There was my hat. Flat and crumpled.

Walking to Paddington Station, I had to pass by the breakfast cafe'. I wanted one last glimpse of the most beautiful woman in the world, and I had an excuse to attract her attention. I had found my hat. Looking in the window, I saw her. I waved my hat energetically until she looked my way. Upon her recognition of me, I emphasized my hat and mouthed, "I found it." She waved back and smiled. I counted my blessings. One, I had found the most beautiful woman in the world. Two, she had my card. Three, there is always a chance she'd call. I had hope.

During my flight to Amsterdam, I had time to reflect on my London campaign. It felt very anti-climactic. Nothing had come of it. The negotiations had been nothing more than senseless chatter and a waste of my time. Abba's billions of dollars worth of looted Nigerian funds had dwindled down to the expense of a breakfast. That was all I got out of Abba and his boys. When I returned to my office I would e-mail Abba and explain how desperately he needed to hire me to write some new material. Their story sucked in a big way. It was stupid. They had a million dollars in a briefcase, and still they needed my eight grand to buy chemicals and pay shipping fees? Along with new material, Abba needed better money managers on his team.

How were they going to wash the smudges off two to three million dollars worth of bills overnight? That would have been ten thousand bills per million. At three seconds each to wash, dry and stack that would have been eight and a half man-hours of repetitive labor. At thirty seconds each that would have been two 40 hour work weeks.

The idea of the scamsters asking for a meager eight grand was chintzy. I had gone all that way and been ready to work a deal, and all they could attempt to scam me out of was a meager eight grand? Five thousand pounds doesn't go far in London. Perhaps it was me? Maybe my attire didn't project wealth. Perhaps they determined that I didn't have much more than eight grand to give them. They would have been right. It would be six months before I could think about financial recovery from this trip. I hadn't recovered financially from last year's excursion to Viet Nam.

Before I left for the airport, I asked Marie if I could use the hotel's computer to send an e-mail to Abba. She arranged it with the hotel manager. I contemplated the e-mail I sent to Abba.

Abba,
> *You know what happened. Explain yourself.*
> *Brian Wizard*

What would he have to say about that?

I had to wing it as soon as I arrived in Amsterdam. I had no accommodations waiting for me. I didn't know how far away the airport was from the city. What I did know was, I was somewhere in the Netherlands. I did have a plan: Get to the city, find a place to stay, and meet with Dr. Samuel.

I hit the ATM at the airport. The Netherlands guilder was going at an exchange rate of about two to one for an American dollar. I took out 300 gulden. It looked like more than $150 U.S. dollars. How far it would take me, I didn't know.

I hate standing in lines, but that's what I had to do at the Visitor's Center. I had no reason to venture past it. It took twenty minutes before I stood in front of an energetic Hollander, whose only goal at that moment was to make my stay in his country a good one.

"Everything in four and five star ratings is booked for the weekend. I could try three star accommodations?" he offered.

"Sure. Once I'm asleep I see no difference in the stars," I told him.

He made reservations for me at the Hotel Amsterdam. "It's close to the city," the agent told me. He sold me a bus ticket and sent me in the right direction.

My drag-along suitcase on wheels made a lot of noise as I walked two blocks from the bus stop to the hotel. It clicked and clacked on every space between the cement slabs that made up the sidewalk. I could have made music with a stick and a white picket fence as I walked along.

My bag was heavy: 30 kilograms, so said the flight receptionist who checked my bag at Heathrow. It was technically ten kilos overweight. She had to put a tag on it stating that it was indeed "HEAVY." Sixty-six pounds. That's why I appreciated the wheels.

At the hotel, it was an altogether different situation. There was no ramp, no elevator, no escalator, nothing but three tall, steep steps that led to the front door. It was almost a vertical accent. I hoisted the "HEAVY" bag three steps by its side handle.

I found the front door locked when I pulled on its handle. I could see people inside standing at the front desk. They could see me. A buzzer rang. It was my cue to act promptly and open the door. Inside, I had to hoist my bag another set of three steps.

Then I met a mimic of Basil Faulty, of the famous British television sit-com, *Faulty Towers*. His words were fast and to the point. "Right then. Follow me." The man, whose name could not compete with the impregnated mental image of Basil Faulty, played by John Clesse, then showed me to Deprivation Chamber #16.

I didn't know anything about the chamber's metaphysical powers until the next morning. I wasn't sure what time I had gone to bed the night before, if it was night. From the moment I woke up to the second I read the data on the face of my watch, I experienced a sensation of timelessness. I had no point of reference for time. I was far from everything that told me the time. Even the time zone was different from London's by yet another hour. Where I live, there is not much sound at night, until just before dawn. Then the vibrations in the air increase for hours until the entire forest is awake and alive with the humming of life's activities.

In Dep-chamber one six, I heard nothing. There was no night. There was no dawn. The last time I had been aware of the exact time was when I was boarding the plane at Heathrow Airport. I let myself hover in that no-time -zone for a moment. Then I looked at my watch. "Ten o'clock!"

I remember the Basil Faulty-like proprietor telling me that breakfast was served between seven-thirty and ten. His madness became evident when I arrived at five past ten.

"You are late!" he snapped. "Are you on vacation? Do you think you at your grandmother's house? Breakfast is over at ten," he scolded.

"I'm still hungry," I told him.

"Sit. Sit down," he demanded.

Once seated I noticed it was a buffet breakfast. I got back up and made the rounds. As I was gathering my meal, more people walked in, later than I. The proprietor took their tardiness as a personal affront. Instead of yelling at them, though, he turned to me, and complained, "You all think I am the enemy. You, you folks who can't follow simple instructions are my enemy." He capped his mad chatter with, "You should all be taken out back and shot!"

"Calm down, Basil," I wanted to say if I could mimic Basil's wife.

Back in Dep-chamber one six, my first question regarding Dr. Emma's scam operation was, had his men received a call from London about me? I dialed Dr. Samuel. The phone rang busy, just as Hamza and Mustapha's did after they realized I was a reluctant player.

I tried to reach him a half dozen times on Sunday. The phone was always busy. The London crowd must have made the call, I deduced.

It wasn't until Monday that I learned I was dialing the number wrong. I was supposed to add two zeros to the number I was dialing, now that I was in the Netherlands. This isn't to say I had spent my time in Amsterdam within the confines of Dep-chamber one six. I had hit the streets.

As mentioned before, Amsterdam is a sensible town. Don't bring a gun, as they are illegal. Bring a desire to perform some sort of business, as all aspects of global trade appeared to be there. Also, bring a desire to relax in a climate of social tolerance, especially when it comes to adults enjoying adult recreation. Various mood enhancers that are illegal in the states are accepted as adult recreation in Amsterdam. I began my Sunday with a trip to a local coffee shop, where I could legally buy some quality hemp prod-

137

ucts over the counter. I ordered a cup of white coffee, then asked to see the menu. On a plastic stand-up display holder I read the hemp menu. Four different types of hash, and several different strains of weed were selling for approximately $12.50 U.S. per two-gram bag.

I asked to see a bag of white hash and a bud of Northern Lights. I was familiar with this Northern Lights strain of cannabis, as it had originated in Northern California. Both products came in small zip lock bags. I chose the Northern Lights for nostalgic reasons. I took my coffee and my pot to a table by a large window that looked out onto the street and a canal. I had anticipated this moment the day before and had already procured a small smoking pipe from a local shop. Of course, there I sat at the table with hot cup of coffee, a small pipe filled with quality bud, and permission to smoke, but no source of fire to light the herbal delight. Some things never change.

Eventually, with my mood enhanced by the rush of caffeine and a mental calm derived from the smoke, I continued my stroll through the streets of Amsterdam. I was feeling social, yet had no desire to stop and carry on a long conversation. I was a walk-by talker, as proven by my encounter with a partially bent-over woman who busied herself rolling up the security blinds over her storefront window. In one hand she held steady a long metal rod that reached to the upper framework of the blinds. Her other hand spun the metal rod in a circular motion, raising the blinds.

"Calling it a day?" I asked her on my approach.

The woman looked up and to her right, with her lovely face expressing curiosity. The question she heard was in complete contradiction to the duty she was performing. "No. Just opening," she responded, as I walked past.

She swung her head around to the left after I had walked behind her, listening to the stranger suggest, "You must admit, it was a good idea."

Her expression held a look of amusement as she realized that I, the stranger who was walking backwards to make eye contact with her, awaited a final retort. "Yes. Closing would be good."

In the early evening of that rainy Sunday in Amsterdam, I came across a juggler. He stood underneath a storefront's overhang. The street traffic had thinned to only a few desperate people. I figured the juggler was performing nothing more than a practice session, especially after I saw him drop one of his hollow, plastic, bowling pin shaped objects. On my approach, I asked him, "Ever whack anyone with one of those pins as they walked by?"

"What do you mean?" he asked, while still juggling.

I spun into place underneath the overhang and pretended to juggle plastic bowling pins. During my rhythmic moves I occasionally reached out to bop an imaginary passer-by. I explained my pantomime. "Juggle, juggle, juggle, bop! Juggle, juggle, juggle, bop!"

The juggler stopped juggling to watch and listen. When I stopped acting, he broke into laughter. "No. I never have."

"Work on it the next time there is a crowd," I suggested, in jest, of course.

I cruised the Red Light District. The girls presented themselves in street-side windows. Some windows were a floor above the sidewalk, while other windows had steps that led to a lower split-level. Window shopping had a new meaning. I don't know why, but I simply couldn't rise to the occasion. The girls looked a wee bit rough. Perhaps I had been spoiled by the beauty of the waitress at the Paddington breakfast cafe'? Perhaps I was not so adventurous due to my dwindling budget? A friend recently asked me, after I told him of this investigation, "Doesn't anything scare you?" I replied, "Yes. Women." Especially professional women in the retail trade of their bodies.

On Monday morning I didn't yet know if Dr. Samuel and I would ever meet. I dialed the number just as I had in London, but without the country code. Still, the phone just rang busy.

There are times when odd problems arise that prevent what you want to happen from happening. I find that if the problem is temporary then time itself may march to the rescue. In that case, I justify procrastination, and distract myself by doing something else. I decided some sightseeing would be good. The Van Gogh Museum would be great!

I had no doubt after a three-hour study of the artist's work that he and I could have easily associated, and supported each other's creative endeavors.

Vinnie's painting depicting three boats on a beach by a river inspired a theme to a short story. Only one boat had a name. It was Amitie, the third boat on the beach. I saw it from the artist's point of view on canvas. Through my creative mind's eye I could see the artist from the vantage point of the boat. I imagined a rough draft of the story.

The tale would first introduce a crew of two sailors as they landed the boat onto the beach from the river. They wouldn't notice anyone on the beach until they began their jaunt to town. That is when they would notice an artist setting up his easel.

They needed a light for their cigarettes, but had no matches. One noticed the artist had a pipe, so they approached him for a light. After the artist accommodated their needs, they went their merry way.

Time passed, the morning departed, early afternoon arrived. As the painter packed away his supplies, the two sailors returned to their boat. As a token of their appreciation for the artist's earlier provision of fire, they brought him a box of matches. This kind deed allowed them a chance to view the artist's work. They were happy to see their boat in the painting.

The story would never divulge the artist's name. Only art lovers who have viewed Vinnie's work would have an appreciation for the story's depth.

Back to work. I walked to the Post Office. I could send a fax to Dr. Emma from there. I wanted to explain to him that I had arrived in Amsterdam, but Dr. Samuel's phone was always busy.

Before you go to the counter for service at the post office, you take a number from a ticket dispenser and wait for the number to come up on an illuminated sign. I had number 31. I took a seat in one of the rows of plastic chairs. The place was filling fast. A woman who had just come in took up a seat next to me. She was number 46. The most recent number served had been 29. I looked at the woman. She smiled. I asked, "Is there a trick to dialing phone numbers that I don't know about? I always get a busy signal."

"You must dial double zero first," she informed me.

"Really? I didn't know that." I gave her my ticket, just as the sign turned to 30. "You're next. Thanks."

I dialed Dr. Samuel's number with a preceding two zeros and he answered.

"Dr. Samuel, this is Brian Wizard."

"Yes, Mr. Wizard. I have been expecting your call."

"I have been calling for days. I just found out about having to add two zeros to the phone number. I kept getting a busy signal."

"I am sorry about that. I should have told you. Where are you?" Dr. Samuel asked.

"I'm downtown Amsterdam," I told him.

"What hotel do you stay at?" he asked.

I didn't want to tell him. If they could have no fixed physical address, then why shouldn't I? "I am close to the Marriott Hotel." I could see the Marriott from the outside public phone.

"You are staying at the Marriott?" Dr. Samuel asked.

"No, but I can see it from this phone booth. It's closer to me than my hotel is at the moment," I explained. "Tell me where you are and we can meet there." I wanted to meet on their turf. I wanted to see a physical address. An address I could summon the police to, if necessary.

"This business does not work like that, Mr. Wizard," Dr. Samuel said in a very stern tone of voice. "You must be at your hotel. I will send my assistant to come pick you up. He will bring you to me."

"Okay, but it's quite far to my hotel. I've been walking for hours."

"Go to your hotel and call me," Dr. Samuel instructed. "What is the hotel's address."

"I don't know it, off hand." I didn't want to give my hotel name and address to this guy, but I could see no way out of it. "I'm staying at the Hotel Amsterdam. Do you know of it?"

"No. My assistant will come by taxi. The driver will know," Dr. Samuel assured me. "When will you be there?"

"Within the hour," I told him. It was only a fifteen-minute walk away. "How long will this transaction take?" I asked.

"Two days," Dr. Samuel told me.

I figured as much. My return to London was late Tuesday evening. I was now running out of budget and time for this investigation. My scheduled flight back to the states was on Wednesday out of London.

I waited on the front steps of the hotel for Dr. Samuel's assistant to arrive. The street became congested with the cars of parents who had come to pick up their kids from the school across the street. This congestion was not going to help Dr. Samuel's assistant's arrival. Luckily, as fast as the congestion began, it ended. Everyone involved had done this before.

A taxi pulled up. A black man in the front passenger seat waved his right hand once. I waved back as our eyes made contact. I climbed into the back seat of the taxi that would take me behind the frontline of this story.

"You are Mr. Wizard?" Dr. Samuel's assistant asked for confirmation.

"I am. You are?"

"Tony," the man replied.

"Where are we going, Tony?" I asked pleasantly.

"To a hotel by the airport." Tony was then distracted by a cell phone call.

Same cell phone communication, and temporary place of business, just like in London. I had no recourse if things went astray. It was the same as the London situation. Only this time I'd be stepping deep into enemy territory.

We drove for a good half-hour along the highway that led to Da Hagg and Rotterdam. The combat-ready lamp remained amber-yellow. I was ready and I was staying ready. The mercury was definitely moving in a redwardly direction. One factor that hindered the turn to red was that we were in a public taxi. Nothing would happen inside the cab.

Finally, we came to a hotel that was only minutes from the airport. I was glad I hadn't known this and booked a room here. I would have spent more time in a hotel room instead of walking the smoke-enhanced streets of Amsterdam.

I followed Tony's lead into the hotel. I scanned the lobby, looking for the bar or restaurant. I noticed neither. Soon we were walking through a maze of hallways. We executed a left turn, went up a few stairs, and made another left turn to walk down a long hallway. Partway down we made a right turn down another long hallway. The further from the hotel lobby we walked, the closer to the back alley we came. I thought that this must be what it felt like to be led to the gallows. Room 541 was our final destination.

Tony knocked on the door. The door swung open. Out from behind the door poked the head of the smallest Nigerian I had seen so far. Tony led the way inside the large, and plush, hotel room. It was large enough to sport a hot tub in its center.

Tony stopped and turned to the smaller man. He introduced me to Dr. Samuel. We shook hands. Doctor Samuel then led me to the far side of the room. On my walk across the room I glanced to my left and snuck a peek inside the hot tub. I noticed a small amount of off-colored water and a tall mound of recently whisked suds on one side. My eyes didn't stay on the tub of water after I caught a glimpse of green to my right. There on the dresser was a haphazardly stacked pile of U.S. bills. Most stacks were $100 bills, some fifties. Paper bands wrapped neatly around the stacks indicated they were all from a bank. It was good to see some money. I wondered what my chances were of walking away with some of it.

Doctor Samuel directed me to a chair positioned next to a large, round, wooden table. As I sat down, I peered through the opened curtain and the glass door behind it. The door led onto the hotel's recreation area. I could see a swing set and a swimming pool. This could be a possible escape route.

Dr. Samuel sat directly across from me. A notebook, a cell phone, pens and a small leather bag cluttered his side of the table. He was wearing a dark-blue suit, with a jacket that appeared a size larger than he might normally wear. I could only assume that the oversized jacket was concealing a pistol.

Tony took up a chair next to the pile of money on the dresser.

"How do you want to do this?" Dr. Samuel nonchalantly asked.

I wasn't sure what he meant. When in doubt, make them laugh. "I'll arm wrestle you for the money on the dresser."

Dr. Samuel did laugh. "No."

"In that case, you'll have to tell me your story."

Dr. Samuel got up from his seat and encouraged me with a wave of his hand to follow him across the room. Partway to the front door he stopped, then bent down to open the lid of a small drag-along suitcase. The display of what seemed to be countless $100 U.S. bills did impress me. This collection made the London boys look cheap.

Doctor Samuel reached under a thin plastic wrap that encased the money and withdrew two one-hundred dollar bills. He handed them to me, as he asked, "See how the serial numbers have a mark over them?"

"I do. Crayon by the look of it." It was true. Each bill had black crayon rubbed over the serial numbers. I looked back at the suitcase. It appeared to bulge at its sides. I wondered if it had a false top, and dirty laundry underneath for bulk. Maybe it *was* full of money.

"This mark makes it impossible for you to spend this money." Dr. Samuel explained, "To remove the marks, each bill must be washed." The doctor never said the crayon marks did anything specific, as the London boys claimed of their anti-detection marks.

What Samuel did next surprised me. He bent over the hot tub and swished the two bills around in the off-colored water, creating more suds. After some finger rubbing and a rinse, the crayon marks disappeared. The bills were wet, but otherwise undamaged.

"I thought you had some girls around here." I cracked a light joke.

"No. This is not water. This is . . ." and I wanted to join in with ". . . special chemical solution," but I held my tongue. Dr. Samuel continued on his own, "special chemical solution."

I did say, "Oh, I see," as if I had never heard that story before.

Dr. Samuel handed me the two wet bills, then redirected my attention to the suitcase. Before he spoke, I noticed something odd. Plastic wrap protected the money from wetness. Ironically, the next step in the process was to wash the money in the special chemical solution.

"This is your money. Five million dollars," Samuel dryly expressed.

I stood there as unmoved as he, as if I had such things given to me on a regular basis.

He fired for effect, "There are six more bags. A total of thirty-two million dollars."

The guy knew how to crawl deep inside the core of my dreams: financing. Previous illusions had now taken physical shape and had a cash value. "Thirty-two million will be deposited into your account within seventy-two hours," he told me.

I was eating this up. It sounded great! It sounded real. I was rich!

"Of course, you can have some of the money within twenty-four hours. A quarter of a million, or even a million," Dr. Samuel pitched, while leading the way back to the round wooden table.

Before I sat down, I held the two hundreds up to the window light. I saw the water-mark, and the small USA 100 bar that runs the narrow width of each bill. They looked real. I kicked myself for not picking up an iodine pen to test the bills. With one swipe you can tell if the bills are fake. The streak will be black if they are counterfeit, yellow if they are real. A slight oversight to be corrected next time. At least I had two hundred- dollar bills

144

from the Nigerians. They would make great souvenirs. I attempted to give them back to Samuel, but he waved his hand to signal that I could keep them. "They are yours," he confirmed, which pleased me. Wet as they were, I set them on the table.

The doctor didn't seem to care what I was going to do with the money. He asked no questions about any rise in my bank's suspicion should my account have a sudden influx of big money. Dr. Emma had told me that all Dr. Samuel would want from me was my signature.

"As I said, all thirty-two million dollars will be deposited into your account within seventy-two hours," Dr. Samuel explained again. "It will first be deposited in a special banking facility. Then wired directly to your account in America."

"Sounds good," I told him. "I don't have to move it around from one bank to another first?"

"No. No need for that," Samuel assured me.

"There is one problem," I warned. "Dr. Emma told me about the Chemical Bank being involved. Is that the bank?"

"Yes, it is," Dr. Samuel confirmed.

"I looked in the yellow pages but did not find a Chemical Bank," I revealed.

"Chemical Bank is a secret bank," the doctor told me, his voice low and serious. "This is what you must do. To receive this money you must become a member of the Secret Bank. This is a secret banking institution. All the rich people in the world have paid to be members of the Secret Bank. Wherever you find rich and powerful people you will find members of the Secret Bank."

Listening to him, I thought, Secret Bank isn't that synonymous with: A stranger's back pocket?

"Tony," Dr. Samuel called to his assistant. "Go get an application."

Tony left the room. An odd thought raced through my head. With Tony out of the room, I might have had time to reach into my carry-on bag and extract my CIA dagger. This hard plastic, three-edged dagger had passed through every airport security scanning device. The scamsters did not frisk me. That did not mean they hadn't scanned me for metal. In one quick move I would plunge the dagger into Samuel's throat with my right hand. With my left I would reach inside his thousand-dollar suit coat and extract his pistol. Then I would decide whether or not to finish him. Whatever took place, my main objective would be to grab my bag and fill it with the pile of cash on the dresser as I worked my way toward the five million dollar bag and the room's front door.

Less than two minutes later, Tony returned. My mad dash for the money would have met with a fiery end, I'm sure. At least I would have Dr. Samuel's hand gun and been able to continue my mad dash, gun a-blazing. I did not know who might have been watching, or what real resistance I would have met. In addition, I could have figured on hotel security and the local police being drawn into the combat. Such a drastic turn of events would have spoiled the memories of this trip to Amsterdam. I would have been a fugitive, on the run in Europe, and unable to return to Amsterdam's liberal coffee shop scene. Also, the alleged five million dollars in the suitcase might have been mostly dirty laundry, and the cash on the dresser could have been counterfeit.

During my mental flash of hands-on combat, Dr. Samuel was talking. I had to ask him to repeat himself. "I was saying, you have to join the Secret Bank in order to receive the money. The membership fee is seventy-five thousand U.S. dollars."

"Only seventy-five?" I asked so dryly that I thought I was going to choke. I swallowed and asked for confirmation. "I'll then have thirty-two million electronically wired to my account within seventy-two hours?"

"Correct. Can you pay the membership fee today?" Dr. Samuel asked with a seriously straight face. Before I could answer, he added, "As I said, you can have some within twenty-four hours, if you like."

"I'd take a million now. Just to cover my expenses for the next month," I told him. I had no doubt that I could enjoy the rest of the winter cruising around the Mediterranean with a million bucks at my disposal.

The reality was more like: For seventy-five grand I could become a card carrying member of the Greedy and Stupid Club. I wondered if I'd be a charter member, so I asked. "How many members have already joined the Secret Bank?"

"I think . . .," and Samuel paused to recollect the appropriate facts and figures for this question. "Twenty thousand, so far. Tony? How many members?"

Surprised to be suddenly brought into the conversation, Tony turned to us with a blank expression. He said nothing for a moment, as he made sure he understood the question. "Yes, about twenty thousand."

Such a deal it wasn't. I remembered how long it would have taken Hamza to wash his meager three million dollars worth of stained money. It would take a small industry to remove 640,000 crayon marks from thirty-two million bucks. That also meant, someone had to mark all those bills. Don't forget the part about drying, stacking and wrapping all the money, too.

"Do you have that much cash available to you today?" Samuel reiterated.

"I have a letter from Doctor Emma. He explicitly states that I have no fees to pay. All you need from me is my signature." I passed Dr. Samuel the faxed memo, after I withdrew it from my carry-on bag.

"There are no fees, per se. This payment is for membership in a very exclusive club. The Secret Bank will securely transfer the money to your account, and they will be with you should you have any problems whatsoever," Samuel told me, with promise in the tone of his voice. He passed me the form Tony had retrieved from another room.

It was a neat form with a bold letterhead, *SECRET BANK*, in large letters. In small letters beneath the form, I read: *Membership Application*. A red center had one-inch white borders all around and white spaces for me to fill with personal details. I could find no phone number or address for the Secret Bank.

I indulged myself with the idea of writing several good scripts that I could sell to all the different scam factions. Secret Bank! Ha! Who would believe in that? No phone. No address. Seventy-five thousand bucks gone.

"The thirty-two million dollars will be deposited into your account within seventy-two hours, and you can have a million dollars tomorrow, as you have requested," Dr. Samuel restated the next-to-the-bottom line.

The bottom line was clearly in place on the bottom of the application form. It read in red ink on the white background:

A FEE OF $75,000 U.S. MUST ACCOMPANY THIS FORM

Taking no chance of a lack of understanding on my part, Dr. Samuel spoke the bottom line for me to hear. "With the paid seventy-five thousand dollar membership fee accompanying the completed application, you will receive an account number. The money will then be ready for deposit into the Secret Bank . . ."

I interrupted with, "The Chemical Bank?"

"Yes, the Chemical Bank," Samuel answered. He continued his final sales pitch, "The Secret Bank will then wire transfer the money into your American bank account."

I had nothing to say. I understood the game. It was clear. I did have one question, though. When do I get my Greedy and Stupid Club membership card?

Dr. Samuel answered my unasked question with, "I will give you a secret code right now. You will use this code in all further communications."

"A secret code for the secret club?" I asked. When do I get the key to the tree house, I silently asked.

"Yes," Samuel said, looking up from the notebook on the table. "Your code number is DS42."

I extracted my note book and pen from my bag, then wrote down my new name: Dumb Shit Forty-two.

While I wrote, Dr. Samuel said, "This is a simple matter. In three days you can kiss all your worries good-bye." Symbolically he kissed the palm of his right hand, then blew the kiss away.

I couldn't help wondering what would happen next if I did pay the money. Would it remain a mystery forever? Would this be the day I lost thirty-two million dollars? I did not have the research budget to splurge on a grand finale. I didn't have a satisfactory conclusion to my investigation.

Then fate stepped it. The Great God of Investigations could no longer sit on the side lines. It too had to know what would happen next if I paid the money. The cell phone on the table rang. Dr. Samuel had the phone to his ear before the second ring. The caller yelled, "Where's my money?"

Dr. Samuel rose from his chair and walked to the far side of the room. This was not a conversation I needed to hear. I couldn't help hearing it, though. The woman's voice, speaking in English, was so loud I could hear most of what she said. "I need that money now. You said . . ."

"Call me back in ten minutes," Dr. Samuel told her. "I am in a meeting. I will explain everything to you when you call back."

There was my conclusion. What happens next is, you wait and wait and wait for the money that never comes. It also meant our business was at an end. The combat-ready lamp remained amber-yellow. I never felt threatened. I would not encounter any hostility here. I would either pay up and leave with high expectations, or I would simply walk away.

"That was the Canadian woman who paid the money on the dresser. She will be receiving a quarter of a million dollars tonight," Samuel assured me. "What about you?"

"Take a check?" I asked, reaching for my jacket's inside pocket.

"No," Samuel said, with a smile. I knew he saw my humor, but he didn't want to show it.

"It will be good in ten days."

"No. We cannot afford a paper trail," Dr. Samuel explained.

"Secret Bank," I stated, with understanding. "No checks. No credit cards. Cash only."

"Yes. We need cash, just like what is on the dresser."

"You said that the money in the bag is mine. I'll take that now, and you can have the seventy-five grand out of it. You'll only have to wire transfer twenty-seven million into my account," I proposed.

"That money must be washed first," Samuel reminded me.

Laundered, I thought. Perhaps when the Nigerians first heard of the scam to launder money they visualized the act of washing clothes. There not being an obvious reason for the cleansing, they invented the crayon marks to make the process worthwhile.

"I was instructed by Dr. Emma that I would not need a large sum of money. Therefore, I don't have any. I guess . . ."

Then the cell phone rang, again. This time Dr. Samuel got up before he put the phone to his ear. Still, I heard the recent Greedy and Stupid Club member yell, "I need my money now! I have a plane to catch!"

Whoever she was, she was presently experiencing the scamsters' final play. All scam victims have a plane to catch. Their vacation from the mundane rituals of making a living is over. They've had their chance to make some easy money by risking their life savings. Now it becomes time to return to work, and start all over.

Samuel assured the woman, "We will be able to pay you your money very soon." He ended his call, then turned his attention back to me.

"You're a businessman," I told him straight, staring eye to eye. "Since I was under instructions not to bring money, perhaps you could make me a personal loan for seventy-five grand today. I'll pay you one hundred and fifty grand tomorrow. That's good business," I assured him.

"I do not have that much money. I am paid a small weekly wage. I cannot help you."

"Well, I'm going to have to return to the states and sell some stuff to raise the capital, I'm afraid," I told him, with disappointment clearly expressed. To myself, I thought, "And write a book about the scam to make a few million honest dollars. Then I'll come back for the sequel."

"How long will this take?" Samuel asked, glancing at his watch.

"Two weeks. A month," I guessed.

"Two weeks would be fine. A month is too long," Dr. Samuel told me.

"I can only do what I can do," I told him.

My host rose from his chair. I followed suit, taking my two hundred-dollar souvenirs off the table. I had to ask, "Can I have a few more of these?" Dr. Samuel's negative head shake meant "No," and I slipped the two bills into my wallet.

"Call me in two weeks," he instructed.

"I will."

"Tony will accompany you back to your hotel." Dr. Samuel offered his hand for a farewell shake. "It was nice to meet you."

"You too. I'll be in touch."

* * *

Returned to Deprivation Chamber #16, I did the math on my expense account. I had enough money to take one more loop around the city. I wanted to treat myself to some of Amsterdam's treats one more time. I found a great bakery for after-coffee desserts.

What I needed the most was a counselor, a therapist, someone, anyone to talk to for the purpose of debriefing. A residual rush of adrenaline had me psychologically hyped into a combat-ready alertness that would not allow me any rest until I had come down. Dep-chamber one six was much too small to hold my expanded sense of combat readiness. I reviewed the events of my latest excursion into the fray of the Nigerian Scam. I had escaped any harm. I had not been ripped off for money, and I had actually come out two hundred dollars ahead. Scammed the scamsters! An investigation doesn't get any better than that. I had to tell all this to someone, so I hit the streets. Who did I find to bear the burden of providing a sympathetic ear? Olaf.

Olaf was a German immigrant. An illegal immigrant who had no papers, and therefore could not work. Hungry and wet, Olaf stood on a curb, panhandling. "Could you spare some money for food?" I heard him ask a couple, as they passed him by.

Olaf saw me coming and stuck his coffee cup in my general direction. "Money for food?"

"Eat pizza?" I asked.

"Yes," the panhandler replied.

"Come on. I saw a pizza shop just around the corner. We ordered pizza and beer, but Olaf gave up the drink and settled for coffee. At a table we sat, and I talked. What I liked about Olaf was, he knew how to listen. I could only imagine that he had a lot of time to listen when he was in prison. He never admitted being in prison. I never asked if he had ever done time. I didn't need to. I could tell on our walk to the pizza parlor that he had done some serious time in jail, with shackles. I walk with the gait of a free man. Shackles restrict the gait of a prisoner. To keep up with me, Olaf had to scurry. His mind would not let him extend his stride beyond the length of the accustomed shackles.

During my informal debriefing Olaf asked questions when I was unclear, and told me he understood when what I said made sense. A pizza later, I had said all I needed to say to bring myself down from my combat-ready mental condition.

Immediate debriefing from combat is a trick that will keep a guy sane. I learned this the hard way after living with the burden of negative psychological conditioning gained during and after my combat experience in Viet Nam.

"I don't think I'd go anywhere with known gangsters," Olaf confessed.

"They gave me two hundred American dollars to listen to their story. It only took a couple of hours," I explained.

151

"For two hundred American dollars I would let them talk to me all day," Olaf admitted.

Olaf also admitted that his presence would hold me back from my walk around town, so we separated at the pizza parlor's entrance. I proceeded to the red light district. I thought one last look at the girls with all this scam business out of the way might be fun. Unfortunately, it was another wet Amsterdam night. The walls of the buildings, the cars, the sidewalks, and the streets, all glistened from a fresh rainfall. I had my umbrella and my hat, so that didn't matter. The weather was not conducive to pleasant strolls along the Amsterdam canals, so the foot traffic was light.

Soon after I entered the district where women sold sexual favors from streetside windows, I experienced real fear. I casually strolled among the glistening concrete, wood and glass of the rainy Amsterdam night. I looked down the street and saw no action, but across the street a small crowd had gathered. Perhaps one of the ladies in the windows was putting on a show. I decided to cross the street to have a look-see.

Amsterdam sidewalks are not very wide. The streets themselves are small. I executed a left oblique turn to cut at an angle across the shiny roadway. Five steps more and I would begin to cross the main thoroughfare. On the third step, I experienced the greatest fear of my journey, and my heart leaped into my throat. My internal combat-ready lamp switched to bright red: Immediate Danger! Every muscle in my body fought my will to continue the trek.

"Whoa, ho-ho-ho!" I said, stopping dead in my tracks. I saw the danger. It only took a nano-second to experience all of this. In a few seconds more I would have realized that what I had thought was the glistening main thoroughfare was actually the shiny-black canal water, preceded by four foot drop below the pavement. I could easily imagine the chaos and confusion I would have experienced had I not stopped in my tracks. There would have been a long moment of terror soon after the commitment of the final step. My body weight would have had no place to go but down. Down to the cold and murky canal water.

EPILOGUE

As it turned out, and I am sure you have figured this out, too, it was all a scam. I could have gone the next step and paid the money if I had been rich, greedy and stupid enough. It might have been a good tax write off.

Fortunately, I returned to San Francisco a tad under budget, not counting the two hundred-dollar bill souvenirs. I was one hundred and twenty-three dollars under budget, to be exact.

Unfortunately, I lost that to another scam. This one was a legal Nevada scam located in the casinos of Reno.

There are some unanswered questions to my investigation like: Whatever happened to the Canadian lady and her money?

Sweetheart, if you are listening, we would all like to hear your side of the story, especially the part not explained here. What happened next?

Tell me this is no scam. I would love to be proven wrong. I would re-title this story as, *The Time I Lost Billions of Dollars.*

Please tell me a happy ending where all your dreams come true.

Otherwise, if you have received an unsolicited letter, e-mail or fax from anyone, anywhere, that tells you they have a few million, or billion, bucks with YOUR NAME ON IT, be wary. Be careful. Be real.

I think Dr. Emma said it best in this fax I found waiting for me at my office.

DR. EMMA JOHNSON BSC., ICAN., MBA.,Ph.D.

EXECUTIVE CHAIRMAN
**CONTRACT AWARD COMMITTEE (NNPC)
IKOYI - LAGOS NIGERIA.
TEL/FAX: 234-90-405-10**

Tel: 234-1-775 0578

February 17, 2000

Dear Mr. Brian Wizard,

Please you have to be careful and very vigilant because according to some security report gathered by my insiders in the system, some people from Nigeria whom I am yet to find out their real identity or intention and whether they are informants, criminals or intelligent bureau / Agents, have infiltrated my communication with you.

These people go about contacting foreign beneficiaries with spurious claims of being the Governor of the Central bank, Minister Taskforce or even the President who poses all powers to release and transfer your fund without delay. *But as you know our funds is in ...*

Within the official quarters it is being suspected that the people may be con-men who want to exhort money from some innocent and unsuspecting foreign contractors.

All their persuasion and sweet promises, to move heaven and earth are simply to lure and obtain some vital information about the deal which they would use against you now or later.
Therefore, I strongly advise you to be on the look out for such faxes / letters.

According to the source of the information, these suspects could also call you from abroad as bank, finance House or Clearing Houses with a claim that your payment has reached their attention and that you are needed to do this or that or even pay some little amount of money to release it.

Take note that they could come in different colours and shades. which ever way, please understand that all are tricks just for the same purpose, either to deceive you and get some information about our deal or to exhort money from you.
So you need to be extremely careful. You should never reply or answer to their faxes or calls, rather, you should send to me such fax / letter the moment you receive them. Never allow anybody to play a fast one on you.

I am concerned about this matter because they might even warn or threaten you not to disclose their information to any other person, but having given you earlier information about unfortunate development, I hope you will not fall into their trap anymore. "To be forewarned is to be formed" and I will not accept any responsibility, which may arise from dealing with such people if you fail to take my advice.

Dr. Emma Johnson

Note: *For avoidance of confusion or doubt, all our communications henceforth shall now bear a personal code: DEJ2000. My phone and fax number remains the same as above.*

Now that you have vicariously lived a "hands-on" experience of the great Nigerian 419 Scam through this story, knowledge is your power to defend yourself. Remember, any percentage of nothing is always nothing.

The scam only works if the intended victims are uninformed of the truth. The scam artists play on our common human characteristics of greed and gullibility. Education is the key. All I can ask of you is to help get the word out. Pass this book along to a family member, or a friend. Better yet, buy as many copies of this book that you can and give them away, or sell them for a profit.

Stand up and be counted as a warrior against this scam. Become an anti-419-Scam activist. Collectively, we can make the call, "GAME OVER!"

Donate copies to your local libraries and learning institutions. Call or write to your favorite radio and television talk shows and request they have me on as a guest to discuss the 419 scam. Join the evolution over the power of the scam. Victory will be OURS.

If you have found this story to answer any questions you may have regarding a recent letter, fax or e-mail sent to you from an unknown person or source from any African country, or if you have found peace of mind knowing now that you have been targeted as a potential victim of the Nigerian 419 Scam, please send your comments to the publisher of this book.

If you want to make your point clear to the scamsters, respond to their offer with something to the effect of, "Thanks, but no thanks. I read the book."

Yours truly,

Brian Wizard

NOTE TO THE SCAM ARTISTS

First, I want to thank you for the excellent fiction you contributed to this story. Congratulations.

Second, I hope my breach of confidentiality doesn't created any hard feelings. After all, you tried to scam me big time for seventy-five grand here, eight grand there, twenty-five grand more with David. Bottom line: I'm a novelist, not a priest.

David, sorry this didn't work out. I truly enjoyed our phone conversations whenever they turned away from the scam and got personal. I think you are too intelligent for all this dirty work. Perhaps a career change would be a good thing.

Dr. Samuel, and Dr. Emma, like I said, I would sell some stuff to raise seventy-five grand for the Secret Bank Membership Fee. If you've read this far, you have just read the "stuff" I am selling. Ironic, isn't it?

Just for grins, someday perhaps I'll swing into Lagos and throw a big party for us all. We'll have fun! I'll bring a copy of my own rendition of how to run a scam. It will be a program with logic and common sense at its core. We'll make trillions!

See you then.
Brian Wizard

PS: Better yet, if you feel the need to get out there and scam someone out of their hard-earned money . . . don't. Go to one of the Amsterdam coffee shops and mellow out, instead.

POSTSCRIPT

The term 419 (four-one-nine) comes from the section of the Nigerian criminal code outlawing fraudulent activities. It has become a part of everyday Nigerian language. As others might say that one has cheated, or stolen, or tricked, or misrepresented, or lied, or conned, etc., a Nigerian will often just use the term "419" to cover all or some of the above activities. This book is an entertaining look at Black Currency 419 operations. Black Currency 419 is actually an updated version of the centuries-old West African con called the Red Mercury scam, in which a special chemical is "necessary" to "clean" (ostensible) bank notes, which have been defaced, in order to make them negotiable. Of course, there is always a problem with the supply of the chemical or with the chemical itself, so the bad guys need money from the target in order to get the job done. Black Currency 419 is the second most prevalent version of the Nigerian Scam. The *most common* version of 419 operations is the Classic 419, basically a money laundering proposal in which the target must supply advance fees in order to free up sequestered funds (which of course don't exist) in return for a percentage of the funds once they are released. Some of the more common "legal" 419 versions are:

Contract Repurchase 419, in which the target thinks he is buying the proceeds of a contract legitimately executed in Nigeria by another firm.

Oil 419, in which the target thinks he is buying a shipment of Nigerian oil at a discounted rate.

Will Scam 419, in which the target is told that he has been willed monies by someone in Nigeria.

Charity 419, in which the target (usually a religious or charitable organization) is told that the persecuted Nigerian Christians or Muslims, etc., depending on the target organization, need to get their money out of the country before it is seized by the Nigerian government or other "hostile" groups. All of these 419s, of course, ultimately require the payment of an advance fee of some sort in order to get the job done.

Nigerian 419 is a global problem, affecting nearly every nation on earth. 419 Coalition has even had reports of 419 operations affecting the island of Yap out in the middle of the Pacific Ocean. One can't get much further from anywhere else than Yap.

Nigerian 419 operations have been running since at least the mid-1980s and conservative estimates of total monies stolen worldwide through 2000 range from $5 billion on up. That's billion with a B. The United States alone has confirmed losses of $100 million per annum, and estimated losses of $300 plus million per annum, according to the U.S. government. And that's just the U.S., there is of course the rest of the world to factor in as well. It has been publicly reported that according to diplomatic sources in Nigeria, Nigerian 419 operations are the third to fifth largest industry in the country. (Oil is of course #1).

What makes Nigerian 419 unique is that there is almost no recourse in Nigeria for the victims. While in the U.S. and other nations there are millions of dollars of 419ed monies seized annually and hundreds of arrests and convictions (mostly of Nigerian nationals, but often of other nationalities as well), in Nigeria for the entire run of Nigerian 419 operations there have been about a dozen convictions to date and monies recovered and repatriated have been minimal. Nigeria has to date functioned, basically, as a safe haven for the 419ers and has done so for many years under several different regimes and forms of government.

It is very necessary to note that the people of Nigeria have been victims of Institutional 419 by successive Nigerian governments in which the rulers have systematically looted the treasury for their own benefit. The most recent Nigerian government under Obasanjo does seem to be making some progress in the recovery of these funds belonging to the Nigerian people, and this is an encouraging sign. However, the regular forms of 419 described above, which are basically conducted by Nigerians on foreigners, continue to date largely unabated.

It is also essential to note that the vast majority of Nigerians at home and abroad are honest, hardworking folks who are justifiably appalled at the damage done to their country and to their reputations by their 419er countrymen. It is unfortunate, and unfair, that these good folks are often subjected to suspicion and harassment as suspected 419ers. But given that one cannot tell a 419er without a program, and there is no program, it is likely that these good people will continue to suffer due to the misdeeds of their countrymen for some time to come. Both the targets of 419 who have lost money and the good people of Nigeria are victims of 419.

Nigerian 419 is essentially one of the most successful and longest running direct mass-marketing campaigns in history, with millions of letters and e-mails arriving into the homes and offices of people and businesses all over the world each year. Losses by individuals often reach into the millions of dollars. According to the targets in several such cases, everything they could possibly check out was checked out. Phone numbers, addresses, work numbers, and job titles of the 419ers were checked.

Some of the targets even held meetings with bona fide Nigerian government officials in bona fide Nigerian government offices where their "deals" were specifically discussed in front of witnesses. Still, they got 419ed. All of a sudden, when push came to shove, the targets realized they had been taken, and nothing was real. The phone numbers were all "fakes" (even those of the main switchboard of the Central Bank of Nigeria obtained from directory assistance where the targets called and got put through to their 419ers at work); the government officials were on Mars the day the meeting was held; the government offices were "rented" by 419ers for the occasion, and nobody can figure out by whom, etc. You get the picture.

Sometimes even after targets have been 419ed for millions of dollars, they continue to believe that their ship will come in, despite being told that they have been ripped off by the 419 Coalition, by the U.S. government, and by everyone else under the sun who knows anything at all about 419 matters.

We here at 419 Coalition call such people True Believers (after an Eric Hoffer book of the same name). And it often seems that the better educated, better traveled, and more successful the target is, the more likely he is to be a money-loser and to become a True Believer. They have to be successful people to have made the kind of monies that they lose, but their egos just won't let them believe that they have been taken. And so they lose more.

Finally, although this book is a light-hearted look at 419, you need to know that a dozen deaths of those targeted have been reported, including that of one American who went to Lagos and apparently refused to go along with the 419ers. They cut off pieces of the man and sent them to his home, with a demand for ransom. After receiving a million dollars in ransom they drove the man, soaked in gasoline, up the street in front of one of the major hotels in Lagos, dumped him out of the car, and set him ablaze. No one knows whether the victim was alive or dead when the Zippo got flicked, but he was certainly dead thereafter. No one was ever caught or charged with this crime. So, be careful out there.

Coordinator, The 419 Coalition.
http://home.rica.net/alphae/419coal/
June 2000

Be one of the lucky readers - book collectors - to own a limited edition of:

BRIAN WIZARD'S TWENTIETH CENTURY ANTHOLOGY
This compilation of work includes:

The Will He Make It Saga, consisting of:

Permission to Kill, a highly acclaimed Viet Nam war story based on Brian Wizard, and his friends, experiences as Assault Helicopter crew members.
Back in the World and **Permission to Live** are two sequels that follow the protagonist of *Permission to Kill*, Willie Maykett, through the next thirty years working through the detrimental aftereffects of his combat experience.
Thunderhawks, the video documentary, composed of actual combat scenes shot by Brian Wizard and his combat peers in Viet Nam.

Heaven On Earth, is a spiritual satire about the Daughter of God's escape from Heaven, in search of true love.

Shindara, a dolphin's tale, set off and on the coast of Australia, and told from the dolphins' point of view. *Shindara* is for the 14 year old in us all.

Brian Wizard Sings for His Supper is a collection of eleven original Brian Wizard songs, written, performed and produced on CD by Brian Wizard and friends.

There will be a limited printing of 100,000 *Brian Wizard's Twentieth Century Anthology*. Each anthology comes accompanied by a signed and numbered Certificate of Authenticity, embossed with the *Brian Wizard's Inc.* corporate seal. This is a book collector's dream come true.

Coming soon! All books, individual or sets, will be available on CD and E-Books.
Order from http://**www.brianwizard.com** with E-commerce: Credit Cards, or Personal Checks, or mail in downloadable order form.

POST-PRESS UPDATE

Since my return from Amsterdam I have been busy with the writing editing and publication of this story. At the same time, the Nigerian 419 Scam machine has been running at full steam. Consequently, I was contacted by four more scam operatives. Collectively, they have added another interesting twist to this story. Unfortunately, at this late date I am not able to add this extra tidbit of entertaining information to this first printing. I will, however, add it to my website for your free perusal. I think this added reading material will make you laugh, plus solidify your belief in the age old adage: *There's no such thing as free money.*

Please visit my website: **www.brianwizard.com** and click on the link that reads: *Nigerian 419 Scam "Game Over!" Post-Press Update.*

The second printing of this book will include what I have had to leave out this first printing.

Another continuation of the *Nigerian 419 Scam "Game Over!"* may also be include on the Brian Wizard website. This link will read: *Hands-on Engagement Three.* This will be an educational experience of a personal nature, specifically designed for those who still don't see the light that emanates from a premeditated scam.

Read the Post-Press Update at:

www.brianwizard.com

Please, tell a friend about this book, and other Brian Wizard novels, artwork, videos and music available from the Brian Wizard website. Handy tear-out informational slips are available on the next page.

Become an Anti-419 Scam Activist by referring this book to everyone you know. Everyone is a target of the Nigerian 419 Scam. Education is the *ultimate weapon* in this war between acceptable and unacceptable business practices. No one likes to be scammed!

If you know of someone who would enjoy Brian Wizard's creative talents, please rip out the information below and pass it on to them.

Brian Wizard is a literary rebel with a clause:

READ MY BOOKS

Visit http://www.brianwizard.com for details on all of Brian Wizard's books, videos, artwork and music. Free Short Stories to read on-line. On-line ordering available with Credit Cards, or Personal Checks. Or, place order by writing to:

Brian Wizard's Inc.

P.O.Box 42

Wallowa, Oregon, 97885 USA

Brian Wizard is a literary rebel with a clause:

READ MY BOOKS

Visit http://www.brianwizard.com for details on all of Brian Wizard's books, videos, artwork and music. Free Short Stories to read on-line. On-line ordering available with Credit Cards, or Personal Checks. Or, place order by writing to:

Brian Wizard's Inc.

P.O.Box 42

Wallowa, Oregon, 97885 USA

Brian Wizard is a literary rebel with a clause:

READ MY BOOKS

Visit http://www.brianwizard.com for details on all of Brian Wizard's books, videos, artwork and music. Free Short Stories to read on-line. On-line ordering available with Credit Cards, or Personal Checks. Or, place order by writing to:

Brian Wizard's Inc.

P.O.Box 42

Wallowa, Oregon, 97885 USA